Teaching & Supporting Learning in Further Education

Second Edition

Teaching & Supporting Learning in Further Education

Meeting the FENTO Standards

Second Edition

Susan Wallace

Learning Matters

First published in 2001 by Learning Matters Ltd, under licence from Limelight Education Ltd.
Reprinted in 2002.
Reprinted in 2003 (twice).
Reprinted in 2004 (twice)
Second edition published in 2005.

British Library Cataloguing in Publication Data
A CIP record for this book is available from the British Library.

ISBN 1 84445 039 2

Cover design by Topics – The Creative Partnership
Project management by Deer Park Productions
Typeset by PDQ Typesetting
Printed and bound in Great Britain by Bell & Bain Ltd, Glasgow

Learning Matters Ltd
33 Southernhay East
Exeter EX1 1NX
Tel: 01392 215560
Email: info@learningmatters.co.uk
www.learningmatters.co.uk

CONTENTS

How to use this book

This book is intended to help all those teachers and student teachers working towards a FENTO (Further Education National Training Organisation) qualification in teaching and supporting learning. Since September 2001, all newly appointed teachers in further education (FE) have been required to hold, or work towards, a nationally recognised (that is, FENTO-endorsed) teaching qualification. Although FENTO itself no longer exists under that name, the requirement and the title of the Standards remain. This means increased numbers of teachers in colleges will be engaged simultaneously in teaching and acquiring a professional qualification. The book is designed to show how these two activities can each support the other. It maps the wide areas of overlap where evidence of sound professional practice can be used to satisfy the requirements of such a qualification. Intending teachers, too, on full-time FENTO-endorsed FE teacher education programmes, such as the PGCE (Postgraduate Certificate in Education) FE or the Cert Ed (Certificate in Education) FE, will find ideas and learning materials to help create opportunities for them to gain and demonstrate the appropriate skills and essential knowledge.

The structure and content of the book are shaped by two main concerns. These are that it should encourage a developmental rather than instrumental use of the FENTO Standards; and that it should emphasise the need to place reflection at the centre of professional practice. It does not aim to provide a history of FE or a guide to the qualifications framework. The further reading at the end of each chapter points out where this sort of information can be found. The purpose of this book is rather to suggest ways in which the skills set out in the standards can be mapped against the teacher's or student teacher's own experience and practice, and to provide case studies, questions, ideas and sources of information that will help them to develop and demonstrate the professional expertise the standards designate as essential skills and knowledge.

Chapters 2–8 each take as their subtitle one of the FENTO key areas. This indicates the broad focus of the chapter but should not be taken to mean the chapter contains specific reference to every skill and knowledge component of that key area. The FENTO Standards are not intended to be applied in this way. That is to say, they should not be used instrumentally as a 'tick-list' of 'competences', but rather as a guide to the standards of professional practice required of a teacher in further education and training. FENTO-endorsed qualifications will have satisfactorily mapped their requirements against the standards, but may have their own emphases or omissions that will have been justified in their rationale. This represents a recognition that standards for professional practice cannot be represented simply or exclusively by a rigid list of knowledge and behaviours. The day-to-day practice of teachers, lecturers and trainers is too varied and disparate for that to be the case. The idea of a minimum standard of good practice is less useful, and certainly less desirable, than a model of reflective, scholarly professional development, underpinned by values such as reflection on practice, collegiality and inclusiveness. This is an argument explored in more depth in Chapters I and 8.

The stages

The standards map three stages in the teacher's professional development: Introduction, Intermediate and Certification. Full-time teachers and those in fractional posts will be required to gain the full Certification stage of the qualification. Part-time teachers will be required to gain the Introduction or Intermediate stage, depending on the extent and range of their teaching. The three stages do not, however, denote different levels of achievement. They are differentiated by breadth of professional activities rather than by depth of reflection, knowledge or expertise. The content of each chapter, therefore, can be applied by the teacher or student teacher to whatever stage he or she is working towards in his or her professional development. The listings at the beginning of each chapter indicate the specific skills and essential knowledge appropriate to each stage; and the Appendix provides a summary, linking skills to the suggested activities.

Skills and knowledge

These listings indicate the skills and essential knowledge which are particularly appropriate to the focus of that chapter, and are intended to help the teacher or student teacher map the contents of the chapter against his or her current needs and professional involvement. They are not, however, intended to be definitive. For example, the reader may find ideas in the chapter which throw light on some aspect of his or her practice which is not listed there but elsewhere. A skill or area of knowledge may be relevant to more than one chapter, or may be more usefully integrated into a topic or activity contained under the chapter heading of a different key area. So, for example, Chapter 2 ('Keeping a journal') does not attempt to cover methodically every skill and essential knowledge descriptor listed in the standards' key area g but, rather, gives guidance on ways in which the teacher or student teacher may demonstrate reflective practice across all the key areas. It is in the nature of professional practice that it is not easily compartmentalised. The listings and the chapter subtitles are intended primarily as a guide, therefore, to help familiarise the reader with the standards and to relate them to the context of day-to-day practice.

For a more systematic mapping, the reader may turn to the Appendix, where the full table of FENTO Standards can be found, mapped against the activities and sources of evidence suggested in this book. Again it must be stressed that this is intended as a means of easy reference only, and should not be used as a tick-list.

The sequencing of chapters and tasks

The sequencing of Chapters 3–8 does not follow any rigid system of progression. We cannot claim that we, as teachers, must be able to plan before we can assess, or assess before we can make an informed choice about what methods to use for teaching and learning. The skills teachers must develop are by their very nature integrated and interdependent; and the process of teacher education may in this respect be described as holistic. Chapters 3–8, therefore, do not imply a modular sequencing of course content and can be read in any order. And, just as with the skills areas of the FENTO Standards, you will find a degree of overlap between chapters. Again we cannot, for example, discuss planning without touching upon assessment, or supporting learners without looking at methods and techniques. Chapter 2, which focuses upon keeping a reflective journal, is, however, placed early in the book in order to establish the importance of reflective practice. The chapters that follow draw and build upon this central aspect of continuing professional development.

In Chapters 2–8 you will find suggested tasks you may choose to work through individually or, if you are lucky enough to be undertaking your professional development as part of a group, you might wish to tackle and discuss as a group exercise. You will also find tasks designated 'close focus'. These usually provide an opportunity for more in-depth reflection and, again, are suitable for an individual or group response. Underpinning the skills and knowledge content of these chapters are the core values of reflection and inclusiveness, which run as a theme throughout the book.

Chapter content

For readers who wish to explore and reflect upon the purpose and the context of the new standards for teaching and supporting learning in FE, Chapter I provides some critical and theoretical background. It presents two arguments which underpin the chapters that follow. One is that it is neither useful nor desirable to interpret the standards in an instrumental way as a tick-list of competencies to be met. The other is that, although the move to consolidate professional standards of teaching in FE is likely also to raise standards of student achievement, student motivation and achievement may depend upon other factors as well. Even excellent teaching will not always guarantee highly motivated, highly achieving students. Unlike all the chapters that follow it, this chapter has a theoretical and academic focus, rather than a practical one. It elaborates specifically upon the FENTO Skills G1b and G1c. Some readers relatively new to the FE sector may prefer, therefore, to begin at Chapter 2 and treat Chapter I as a final chapter which draws together some of themes raised throughout the book about professionalism, scholarship and the post-compulsory system.

Chapter 2 focuses upon reflective practice. This is one of the core values which underpin the standards. It is used, therefore, as a starting point for the practical content of the book. Using extracts from teachers' journals, it explores what constitutes reflective practice and why this is important to the teacher's professional development. In the process of analysing journal extracts, it shows how to structure reflective writing in such a way as to help review and revise future practice.

Chapter 3 examines how we plan the teaching and learning experiences of groups and of individuals. Continuing the theme of reflective practice, it uses journal extracts and learning plans to illustrate some of the important features of good lesson planning and warns against some of the pitfalls. It takes a problem-solving approach, inviting the reader to analyse and comment on examples of planning and to undertake some planning of his or her own.

Chapter 4 engages with two key areas of FENTO skills: assessing the needs of learners and providing them with support. Based around a case study of one teacher's first encounter with a particular group of students, it encourages the reader to analyse this lesson (from the teacher's first-person account of it) in terms of opportunities for identifying and meeting the needs of the students. There is also an evaluation of the teacher's account in terms of whether it meets the criteria of reflective practice.

The theme of Chapter 5 is assessment of student achievement. It takes a case-study approach in illustrating and examining some basic assessment theory, and it poses practical questions to the reader about validity, sufficiency and reliability. The theme of inclusiveness as a core value is particularly emphasised in this chapter, as it is in Chapter 6, which focuses on methods and strategies of teaching and learning. Here the issue of using methods appropriate to students' learning styles and needs is explored through the experiences of a student teacher and a teacher recently appointed to a full-time post in FE. Again, the reader is presented with tasks and questions based upon these examples of practice.

Chapter 7 focuses upon how we manage learning and motivate students. It takes as its starting point a tutor's evaluation of a student teacher's lesson and encourages the reader to identify what could have been done to improve student motivation. It examines some basic learning theory and shows how this can be applied to the design of teaching and learning materials.

The final chapter to be based explicitly on the FENTO skills is Chapter 8. It combines the key area of meeting professional requirements with the core values of professionalism and scholarship. Using extracts from historical and fictional texts, it encourages the reader to reflect upon professional values and practices, and to begin to identify and articulate those values which inform his or her own professional practice and which are likely to influence and direct his or her future professional development.

Chapter 9 looks at the language and literacy elements of the Minimum Core, and shows how the teacher's grasp of this aspect of the Core is essential to developing the Key Skills of their students, particularly in Communication. It includes some examples and exercises which will enable the teacher to evaluate their own key skills against what is demanded by their teaching, as required by section GI of the standards. Chapter 10 provides a summary of the theories of learning covered in the preceding chapters, and suggests some accessible sources for further reading and reflection.

Finally, the Appendix provides a comprehensive system of cross-referencing the standards to possible sources of evidence from the teacher's or student teacher's current practice; it also identifies overlaps and similarities in requirements from different key areas.

1 SETTING THE STANDARD: THE BACKGROUND TO THE STANDARDS FOR TEACHING AND SUPPORTING LEARNING IN FURTHER EDUCATION

This chapter introduces the background and context to the FENTO Standards and discusses the implications, uses and the limitations of such a framework. As well as providing a context for the chapters which follow, it sets out to model and explore the FENTO core values of reflection and scholarship. It argues it is these core values that transform a taxonomy of required skills into a framework for professional development. References made in the text are listed in full at the end of the chapter for readers who wish to explore some of these issues further. As well as providing a context for all the areas of skills and knowledge, this chapter is of particular relevance to skills G1b and G1c.

Initial teacher training in FE

Surprisingly little has been written about the perceptions and experiences of teachers new to the FE sector in comparison, for example, with studies of newly qualified or trainee secondary teachers. Such recent literature as exists makes interesting reading for the teacher or student teacher new to FE. McKelvey and Andrews (1998), for example, set out to discover which aspects of their new role trainee teachers in FE found most attractive. What would be fascinating to read, however, is an account by such teachers (at the very beginning of their careers) of the qualities and skills they believe make for effective teaching. How do we define an effective teacher? What are the skills and qualities in which we might reasonably expect them to be competent?

FENTO's development of standards for the qualification of new and inservice FE teachers (FENTO, 1999) is an attempt to address this very question. It reflects the target set in The Learning Age Green Paper (DfEE, 1998) that all FE lecturers teaching full time or with substantial part-time hours should undertake a professional teaching qualification. In The Learning Age, this is presented as a means of improving standards of provision and achievement in FE. The FE Standards Fund, announced by the Secretary of State for Education at the Association of Colleges' (AoC) annual conference in 1998, is targeted specifically at improving the standards of teaching in FE; at ensuring that FE teachers update their subject skills; and at disseminating good practice. Despite such good practice, claimed the Secretary of State, 'there is also too much poor or inadequate teaching' (Blunkett, 1998: 2). The development of the FENTO Standards the following year reflects this strategy of addressing student performance in FE by focusing on teachers and their teaching. In this context, the requirement for all teachers to be qualified to an appropriate and specified level seems a sensible way forward. However, we should bear in mind that the raising of standards in FE may be a more complicated business than this one proposed solution implies.

The FENTO Standards set out for us a comprehensive range of skills ordered under the following headings:

- assessing learners' needs;
- planning and preparing teaching and learning programmes for groups and individuals;
- developing and using a range of teaching and learning techniques;
- managing the learning process;
- providing learners with support;
- assessing the outcomes of learning and learners' achievement;
- reflecting upon and evaluating one's own performance and planning future practice;
- meeting professional requirements.

All these are essential to the teacher's role. The final two, we might argue, define the professional nature of teaching: professional practice based upon reflection and self-imposed standards. There are, of course, difficulties presented by a list like this, as any teacher educator will tell you. One is the difficulty of sequencing. Can one logically expect a student teacher to plan his or her lessons effectively before he or she has covered the principles of assessment, or methods, or how to support learners? Can a student teacher make informed choices about methods before he or she has learnt to plan? And so on. Another difficulty is presented in the very process of separating out these different aspects of the professional role. For example, might not 'Managing the learning process' be thought to subsume many of the other skills areas, such as 'Providing learners with support' and 'Assessing learners' needs'? The answer seems to be that these are skills areas which will be revisited repeatedly in the course of the teacher's professional development, each time with increased depth and confidence.

In addition to these skills areas it has been a requirement since September 2004 for all trainee FE teachers to demonstrate possession of the Minimum Core (SVUK 2003) — the term given to a set of skills and related understanding in language, literacy and numeracy — necessary to support the key skills and wider development of learners from diverse backgrounds.

Stages of professional development

In the Standards, the model of professional development is represented by the three stages: Introduction, Intermediate and Certification. The stages are not to be interpreted as levels. That is to say, all three stages operate at the same academic level. A teacher in FE, contracted to teach a substantial number of hours and working towards the Intermediate qualification, will be working to the same standard as the full-time or student teacher working towards the Certification stage or the part-time teacher who teaches one evening class a week and is working towards the Introductory stage of the qualification. What will differ here is the range of teaching experience upon which he or she will be able to draw and through which he or she will be able to demonstrate the designated skills. It follows, therefore, that the range of skills required for the Certification level is wider than that required for the Introduction or Intermediate stages but that those skills common to all three stages must be demonstrated to the same standard. The stages mark an expansion in the teacher's range, scope and experience rather than represent increasing levels of difficulty.

There are apparent contradictions (but also interesting parallels) here with Gregorc's (1973) theory that teachers' training needs change in accordance with their developmental stage. Gregorc describes four (rather than three) stages of professional development. These are 'Becoming', 'Growing', 'Maturing' and 'Fully functioning'. The developmental needs he identifies for the first stage – focusing upon the use of methods and resources and the skills of planning – might be referred to as a 'survival kit' for teachers and roughly correspond in scope to the Introduction stage as set out by FENTO. In Gregorc's next phase, 'Growing', the teacher's development needs are for consolidation and expansion of these skills and strategies, just as the Intermediate stage consolidates and expands upon the skills applicable to the Introduction stage. In the third phase, however, which Gregorc labels 'Maturing' and which involves strong professional commitment, increased willingness to experiment and an ability to tolerate ambiguity, the teacher's developmental needs move out of the purely operational sphere and into an area much more difficult to express in terms of knowledge and skills. This is what Gregorc says about this stage of a teacher's development:

> 'the teacher comes to realise … that humans learn from many sources and in many ways. When his students fail to attain valid objectives … he examines his objectives, and alters his techniques, materials, and attitudes about roles played in the education process.' (1973: 4)

Although written over a quarter of a century ago, this seems to me an adequate description of what differentiates the FENTO Certification stage from the two earlier stages, particularly when we bear in mind the emphasis, expressed in the FENTO core values, upon reflection and scholarship.

For Gregorc, however, this need not be the final stage in the teacher's potential development. He suggests a fourth, 'Fully functioning', phase, where the teacher has developed a high level of self-direction and astute skills of self-evaluation based upon self-referenced norms. Here the teacher's needs move definitively into the area of self-development and will lead the teacher to seek continuing opportunities for personal and professional growth. This may serve to remind us – if indeed we need reminding – that FENTO's Certification stage should not be taken as the apex of the teacher's professional development but rather as a preparation for continuing professional development and growth.

The parallels between the FENTO stages and Gregorc's phases provide us with a useful perspective on two important issues. The first we may refer to as the issue of 'bottom lines and ceilings'. A key aspect of Gregorc's stage theory is that each phase may represent the ceiling of a particular teacher's development. That is, the teacher may get 'stuck' there, for whatever reason, and never progress beyond it. The FENTO Standards are operating within a different paradigm, although on the surface this may not be immediately apparent. According to FENTO, as we have already seen, the teacher will work towards the stage of the qualification appropriate to the range and scope of his or her teaching, rather than that dictated by his or her 'ability' or potential for development. The only sense in which the teacher can become 'stuck' is if the range and scope of the teaching experience available to him or her remain limited. This is an important distinction to make.

The second issue Gregorc's theory may serve to illuminate is the danger of viewing the FENTO skills as a set of competencies that can be used as a tick-list to assess whether or not a teacher's performance is adequate. Many of the qualities Gregorc identifies as integral to the Maturing and Fully functioning phases would arguably slip right through a net of competencies, however fine the mesh, and be lost. Qualities such as reflection, motivation, commitment and integrity, for example, are difficult to square with a skills-based qualification; and yet it is clear, both from the statement of core values and from areas of the standards such as 'Meeting professional requirements', that FENTO intends these qualities to be embedded within the standards at all three stages. The danger, of course, is that the skills do look like competencies.

Why we shouldn't confuse skills with competencies

It has been argued that the FENTO framework has some conceptual flaws. One of these is that it fails to designate the level at which the skills should be achieved, thus creating a semantic confusion by the very use of the word 'standard' (Bleakley, 1999). This is an interesting point. But let us imagine for a moment that the skills descriptors were sufficiently detailed – by the addition of performance criteria and range statements, for example – as to specify exactly a 'standard' as that term is used in the current vocational qualifications framework. What we should have then would be a set of competencies – a National Vocational Qualification (NVQ) for FE teachers – rather than guidelines appropriate to the development and qualification of a body of professional practitioners. A central facet of the FENTO Standards is the claim that they are flexible and constitute guidelines rather than a framework to be rigidly imposed (Windmill, 2001). For example, providers of FENTO-endorsed programmes may justifiably step outside the guidelines in order to meet local needs (ibid.).

On the other hand, some argue that the standards are nevertheless too prescriptive and that their instrumental nature is consistent with what Reeves (1995: 105) refers to as 'a narrow and inappropriate model of education and training ... which has reduced individual opportunity for educational self-realisation'. Certainly one might argue that although practitioners are encouraged to be reflective, it is not clear whether or how credit is given for the propositional knowledge and resulting professional development arrived at through such reflection. However, as we saw from Gregorc's theory, these elements of professional self-actualisation may not be appropriate qualities for assessment in any traditional sense. To 'give credit' for them within a qualification framework is surely to reduce them to an instrumental function within that framework – and such instrumentalism is the very target at which such critics have aimed their sights.

What is the problem, then, with applying competence-based, 'can-do' frameworks to teacher education and professional development; and why is FENTO concerned to stress that the standards should not be used in this way? After all, many teachers in FE are teaching and assessing on competence-based programmes and are therefore familiar with this model. Part of the answer can be found, I think, in the experience some FE teachers have already had with the NVQ model of teacher development. With the introduction of NVQs came the requirement that all assessors provide evidence of their competence in line with the Training and Development Lead Body's (TDLB) Units D32 and D33. Teachers were required to attend training sessions and compile portfolios of evidence to demonstrate their skills as assessors. It would be an understatement to say this was not well received. The argument was that these TDLB Standards had been developed to meet the training needs of workplace supervisors who had not previously taken on an assessor's role, and were an unnecessary imposition on experienced and qualified teachers. When the same requirement was made of GNVQ teachers, resistance by teachers in schools was followed by the development of the GNVQ Planning and Assessment Units, which were set out like GNVQs, still required the teacher to compile a portfolio of evidence, but were perceived by many as being more developmental and helpful to the teacher new to GNVQs. The instrumental nature of the TDLB units – the requirement to 'tick boxes' to show the teacher was doing something he or she already knew how to do – was resisted partly because it was not seen as helpful. In any FE department you will probably be able to find someone who, although an excellent teacher and assessor, still has an unfinished portfolio of D units.

There are three major arguments related to using 'tick-list' assessment in a teacher development context, and they may be summarised like this:

- teachers may be at different stages of development or involvement and have different needs and aspirations, of which a common programme of competencies might meet only the most basic;
- the NVQ model of competency statement is emphatically employer-led rather than allowing for self-evaluation, reflection upon practice or the setting of self-referenced norms;
- an emphasis on teacher 'performance' may distract from the importance of the teacher-learner relationship and encourage the concept of the passive learner.

The first two issues, of differentiation and reflective professional practice, we have touched upon already. We now need to look at the third – the issue of the teacher–learner relationship.

The teacher–learner relationship

In taking as a starting point the skills and behaviours required in a teacher, we should not lose sight of an equally valid question: what do we hope will result from the interaction between teacher and student? Whatever the answer is, there is no reason why its effects should be confined to the student. The equation that has the teacher as subject and the student as object only encourages the idea of the active teacher and the passive learner. This is what Freire (1972) refers to as the 'banking' concept of education, where the learner becomes the receptacle for knowledge, skills and attitudes – all mediated through the educator who, apparently, remains unchanged by the process.

One way out of this mindset is to make a semantic escape, as Carl Rogers (1983) does when he discards the term 'teacher' and uses instead 'facilitator of learning'. The qualities Rogers argues are desirable in an effective 'facilitator' are very far from skills-based to the extent one could question whether they could be 'taught' to teachers at all. The desirable outcome of the facilitator-student relationship is, in Rogers' view, mutually inspirational:

> '[T]he initiation of such learning rests not upon the teaching skills of the leader, not upon his [sic.] scholarly knowledge of the field, not upon his curricular planning, not upon his use of audio-visual aids, not upon the programmed learning he utilizes, not upon his lectures and presentations No, the facilitation of significant learning rests upon certain attitudinal qualities which exist in the personal relationship between the facilitator and the learner.' (1983: 121)

That list, which Rogers reeled off 20 years ago, could almost be a paraphrase of the FENTO skill areas, and yet he is claiming that none of them is more important to the effectiveness of the learning process than the relationship – of trust and respect – between the teacher and the students.

Now, of course, fashions come and go in education as in other areas of human affairs. We shall see this vividly in Chapter 8, where we shall also encounter Freire and Rogers again. These ideas – that relationship is central to the teacher-learning process and that the teacher is changed by this process, just as the learner is – are at present less fashionable than they were 20 or 30 years ago. We talk of the teacher as 'delivering' the curriculum, handing over learning to the student, in an image reminiscent of Freire's 'banking' metaphor. It seems safe to assume that the rise of competence-based models of education and training has contributed to this change, arising as they do from the instrumental view of education as a process designed wholly or in part to meet the needs of employers and the economy. It is interesting to see how the FENTO Standards have, nevertheless, gone some way towards accommodating models of teaching and learning which acknowledge the importance of the teacher-learner relationship and the way in which the reflective teacher learns and is changed in the process of this interaction. This is particularly evident in parts of the skills areas A, E, G and H: 'Assessing learners' needs'; 'Providing learners with support'; 'Reflecting upon and evaluating one's own performance'; and 'Meeting professional requirements'. It is also evident in the title, which refers not only to teaching but also to supporting learning.

In the early days of the National Council of Vocational Qualifications (NCVQ), before the establishment of the Qualifications and Curriculum Authority (QCA), and when the drive towards competence-based education was at its height, providers of postgraduate initial teacher training programmes for FE were encouraged to conform to the competence-based model. One such programme included amongst its list of competencies 'Looks after small laboratory animals'. This requirement sounds bizarre; and it also serves to illustrate precisely why teacher education and the competence-based model do not sit easily together. On the one hand it is a specific requirement which cannot possibly be of relevance to all, or even most, teachers but has to be included on the grounds it is essential for some. On the other hand, for those to whom it is relevant, it is not specific enough. It is not specified to standard. It might be taken to involve anything from simply seeing that the small animals don't starve, to providing them with long sessions of grooming and displays of affection.

By resisting the competence-based model, the FENTO Standards avoid both these traps. The claim to flexibility means, in theory, that every teacher need not cover every skill, if exceptions or substitutions can be justified; and the avoidance of prescriptive standards for each skill allows for a developmental, spiral curriculum, where the teacher may return to the same skills area several times, on each occasion developing further in confidence and scope.

The current context of FE

As we saw earlier, the FENTO Standards for teaching and supporting learning were designed as part of the initiative to raise standards in FE. It is important, however, we do not lose sight of the overall context in which FE teachers operate. If we do so, we risk falling into the trap of assuming that the quality of teaching is the only problem that needs to be addressed if we are to raise standards of achievement. However reasonably it is expressed, this assumption presents a deficit model of teachers and teaching which serves to perpetuate what Ball (1990) has called a 'discourse of derision'. Setting and acknowledging high standards for the teaching profession in FE are to the benefit of everyone, not least we professionals ourselves. But it would be foolish to assume this alone is the answer to raising standards of student achievement in FE.

If we put teacher performance aside for a moment, what other factors might be serving currently to depress the levels of achievement in FE? Or, to put it another way, what factors, other than the quality of teaching, would tend to affect students' motivation detrimentally? We shall consider three possible culprits here and, in doing so, will take the opportunity to explore some of the policy frameworks within which FE currently operates.

It has been argued, for example by Reeves (1995), that the dominance of the work-related qualification system – the competence-based model discussed earlier – has served to make the FE curriculum less stimulating and enjoyable for the students. The imperative to repeat and acquire skills in a routine very much like that of the workplace may lead students who assume no pleasure is to be gained from work to apply that assumption equally to their education. The expectation is that their effort will be rewarded by accreditation, but not by any enjoyment of the learning itself. This is compounded by the knowledge that, in the current employment market, even if they gain their qualification this will not necessarily give them access to a job. Some researchers, like Ainley and Bailey (1997), claim the expansion of FE and post-16 education and training in general may be seen as a means of occupying young people who are not in employment. The corollary of this is that some students may be staying on in education not by choice but because it is their last resort. It can also mean that students who are perfectly aware their prospects of employment are poor may find themselves on 'vocational' courses preparing for a job they know they are unlikely to be offered. These are brutal arguments. But they are arguments of which the FE teacher needs to be aware. In this context, the question the professional must ask is: given all this, how do I go about motivating these students to engage with, and take pleasure from, their learning? To do this they must be clear that lack of student motivation is not always the teacher's fault.

Another contextual issue which may impinge upon student motivation and achievement is the growing emphasis in FE upon competition and market forces. Since the Further and Higher Education Act 1992, the FE sector has shifted from the strategic regional planning of its provision to a purchaser-provider model. Indeed, it would appear the effects of a policy of free market competition can be more readily observed in FE than in any other sector of education (Ainley and Bailey, 1997). Although the declared purpose of introducing competition is to bring about a raising of standards (the college must ensure its provision is good if it is to compete successfully for students), this market model may have other effects too. One of these is that the concerns of college senior managers and of college lecturers are likely to diverge; the lecturers focusing on students and curriculum while their managers are obliged to focus increasingly upon competition and matters of finance (Ball, 1994). The policies necessary to ensure survival in a competitive market may include increased class sizes, increasing use of resource-based learning and a consequent reduction in the quantity, if not quality, of teacher–student contact. This may well affect the quality of the students' learning experience and consequently their level of motivation and engagement with their learning. If we add to this the financial pressures the market exerts upon colleges to recruit and retain high numbers of students, we can recognise the possibility that some students at least may find themselves recruited on to courses which do not necessarily meet their needs. We can recognise that it could also – although we would hope it does not – lead to tolerance of students who disrupt the learning of others because of pressure to retain viable numbers.

A third factor, which links the work-related qualification system and the pressures of the market, is the use of performance indicators (PIs) as part of the funding mechanism for FE colleges. PIs are a measuring of 'input' and 'output'. In simple terms, this means the student enrolments and the qualifications gained – one way of assessing whether the college is giving value for money. But an emphasis on input and output leaves out the middle of the equation – what we may feel to be the important bit – the process of teaching and learning, other than to decide whether it is cost-effective. Now clearly, enrolment, retention and qualification rates will not tell us everything we need to know about the quality of learning provision. PIs can only be applied to what is easily measured. We have seen this already in relation to competence-based assessment. Teaching and learning represent a complex process.

Embedded in that process are the factors which may encourage or discourage student motivation and engagement. These cannot be assessed by PIs. Moreover, there may be contradictions inherent in the pressure on colleges to attain both high retention and high achievement rates, because students who find a course too difficult would normally drop out. Similarly, there may be difficulties in simultaneously raising achievement and widening participation because widening participation implies the recruitment of, among others, students who may experience difficulties with learning (Perry, 1999).

Since the 14-19 Education and Skills White Paper (DfES 2005) the decision to open up FE provision to 14–16-year-olds has had a profound impact on the working lives of many teachers in FE. Tasked with teaching and supporting the learning of an age group that had hitherto been accommodated within compulsory education and working to the National Curriculum, some FE teachers have understandably felt concern not only at their lack of previous training or experience with Key Stage 4 pupils, but also at their continuing lack of parity with teachers in schools working with similar groups. This is an issue which is not likely to go away. In the 2005 General Election all three major parties declared in their manifesto the intention to incorporate the option of vocational education into the curriculum of all 14-year-olds for whom it might be appropriate.

A programme of teacher education for FE, at whatever stage of teacher development it is aimed, will require that the teacher or student teacher has a clear grasp of the current topography of the FE sector and the ways in which policy impinges upon and shapes practice. To this extent the issues we have just briefly explored are critical in that they form part of the context within which the aspiring professional will be operating. An exploration of such issues, I would argue, is entirely within the spirit of the FENTO core values of scholarship and reflection upon practice.

Conclusion

The strength of the FENTO Standards as a framework for teacher education lies in their flexibility and their emphasis upon the learner. The skills and knowledge they present as essential to the professional FE teacher can be visited and revisited, refined and extended as the teacher gains in experience and confidence. Their core values establish a pattern of self-motivated professional development and reflective practice designed to continue long after the initial qualification is achieved. Most of all, they do not dictate one particular approach or style as being 'correct' or 'desirable'. The teacher is encouraged to identify and explore his or her own strengths and weaknesses and to develop his or her professional role as a manager of learning in ways with which he or she feels comfortable. But teachers are also encouraged to extend their range and repertoire as their confidence grows.

Handal and Lauvas (1987), Norwegian educationalists and advocates of reflective practice involved in inservice education of teachers at various stages, provide a clear summary of why this flexibility is so important:

'*Teachers who have learnt only to accept one model of teaching as the right one will more easily run the risk of either becoming rigid and static in their teaching, or becoming passengers on any educational bandwagon that happens to pass by.*' (p. 22)

Further reading and references

Ainley, P. and Bailey, B. (1997) *The Business of Learning: Staff and Student Experiences of FE in the 1990s*. London: Cassell.

Ball, S. (1994) *Education Reform: A Critical and Post-Structural Approach*. Buckingham: Open University.

Ball, S. (1990) *Politics and Policy Making in Education: Explorations in Policy Sociology*. London: Routledge.

Ball, S. et al. (2000) *Choice, Pathways and Transitions Post-16: New Youth, New Economies in the Global City*. London: Routledge Falmer.

Bleakley (1999) Are the FENTO Standards up to standard? Paper presented to the FEDA Research Conference, Cambridge, 9 December.

Blunkett, D. (1998) Speech to Association of Colleges' Annual Conference, *Reform* 1999 (1), p. 2.

DfEE (1998) *The Learning Age: A Renaissance for a New Britain*. London: HMSO.

DfES (2005) *14-19 Education and Skills*. London: HMSO. www.dfes.gov.uk/publications/14-19educationandskills

FENTO (2000) *Standards for Teaching and Supporting Learning in FE*, www.fento.org.

Freire (1972) *Pedagogy of the Oppressed*. Harmondsworth: Penguin Books.

Green, A. and Lucas, N. (eds.) (1999) *FE and Lifelong Learning: Realigning the Sector for the Twenty-First Century*. London: Institute of Education.

Gregorc, A. F. (1973) Developing plans for professional growth, *NASSP Bulletin*, December, 1973 (1–8).

Handal, G. and Lauvas, P. (1987) *Promoting Reflective Teaching*. Buckingham: Open University Press.

McKelvey, C. and Andrews, J. (1998) Why do they do it? A study into the perceptions and motivations of trainee FE lecturers, *Research in Post-Compulsory Education*, 3 (3), pp. 357-68.

Perry, A. (1999) Performance indicators: measure for measure or a comedy of errors? Paper presented to FEDA Research Conference, Cambridge, 9 December.

Reeves, F. (1995) *The Modernity of Further Education*. Bilston: Bilston College Publications/Education Now.

Rogers, C. (1983) *Freedom to Learn for the 80s*. London: Merrill.

Smithers, A. and Robinson, P. (eds.) (2000) *Further Education Re-formed*. London: Falmer Press.

Windmill, V. (2001) Address at the seminar on FENTO Standards, Nottingham Trent University, 26 January.

Wymer, K. (1996) *Further Education and Democracy: The Community College Alternative*. Wolverhampton: Bilston College Publications/ Education Now.

2 KEEPING A JOURNAL: REFLECTING UPON AND EVALUATING ONE'S OWN PERFORMANCE AND PLANNING FOR FUTURE PRACTICE

This chapter explains how to keep a reflective journal of your teaching and learning experiences and the advantages of doing so. It also explains how a reflective journal can be used to demonstrate you are meeting the FENTO Standards in skills and knowledge relevant to your stage. Following the advice of this chapter, you should be able to provide evidence that meets at least the following standards.

→ **Introduction stage**
  Skills: A1a, F2c, F2d, G1i, G3a, H1c

→ **Intermediate stage.** All the above, plus
  Skills: E4d, G1b, G1d, G1f, G2c, G3b, G3d, H1a, H1e, H1h

→ **Certification stage.** All the above, plus
  Skills: B3f, D7f, G1e, G1g, G1h

→ **Essential knowledge**
  A range of essential knowledge, which is likely to include some areas listed under c1, c3, d1, g1, g2, g3, h1, h2

It is important to bear in mind that the list above is for mapping and guidance. It is not intended as an instrumental 'tick-list' but as an aid to professional development. Remember, too, that these are stages, rather than levels. This means that the depth and quality of reflection are expected to be the same at all three stages but that the range of opportunities for reflection will extend with the teacher's widening experience as he or she moves through the stages from Introduction to Intermediate to Certification.

Why keep a journal?

Socrates claimed that, '*The unexamined life is not worth living*'. All very well for Socrates, you might think. Perhaps he had more time on his hands than an FE lecturer or a student teacher. But the principle is an important one, particularly when we are engaged in teaching and learning. If we don't examine our experiences and reflect on them in a constructive way, how will we learn from our successes and our mistakes? This is why reflective practice is one of the core values informing the FENTO Standards. When our working lives are crowded with incidents and we are constantly hurrying on to the next class, the next meeting, the next project, our focus is usually on planning (or worrying about) what's happening next. This gives us little opportunity or inclination to examine, in any constructive way, what has just passed.

During the morning you may have prepared and taught a lesson which succeeded in every way: you enjoyed it, the students enjoyed it and they achieved the required learning outcomes. Or you may be trying to put behind you one of those lessons which – although it was with a similar group of students – felt like a disaster: mobile phones ringing, students coming in late, the big lad with the nasty sense of humour making sure no one stays on task for long. How do you improve the chances of reproducing more lessons like the first and take measures to avoid more going the way of the second?

This is where keeping a reflective journal can help. You ask yourself: what were the factors that made that first lesson a success? Was it simply that the students were in a positive mood? If so, how could I recreate that? If not, was it something I did that I could do again? And if I had that second lesson to teach again (perish the thought!), is there anything I could do differently – something I did in the first lesson – in order to keep the students more focused on achieving the learning outcomes?

It isn't for nothing that the FENTO Standards place particular emphasis on reflective practice. As professionals in the field of teaching and learning, we can't improve our practice as teachers unless we set ourselves constantly to learn from it. The reflective journal will help us to do this.

What's the difference between a log, a diary and a reflective journal?

A log is usually a factual record of events. A ship's log, for instance, will give a brief day-by-day account of position, weather, speed and heading, with an occasional mention of significant events: another ship sighted or the ship's cat dies. If you were to keep this sort of factual account of your activities it wouldn't qualify as 'reflection'. It would describe the framework of your day, perhaps, but provide no analysis of your experiences and no reminder to yourself of what you think about them and what you might have learnt from them. Even Captain Kirk, whose starship's log is less terse and infinitely more eventful than most, gives only an account of events. His moments of introspection are rare. His log would be of little use to him as evidence of meeting the FENTO Standards of professional reflective practice.

A diary, on the other hand, can serve many purposes. At one extreme it may be used as an outlet for creative writing; at another it may simply be used to record appointments. It may be used to capture or express powerful emotions, or – as in the case of my cousin, whose diary entry for one week read: 'Went to Egypt. Saw pyramids' – it may not.

A reflective journal may be used for all these purposes – to log events, to describe circumstances, to vent feelings – but it will also, *and primarily*, be used to record and reflect upon incidents and experiences from which something useful can be learnt that will help us to develop and enhance our professional practice.

So what does being 'reflective' really mean?

The best way to explore this question is to look at some extracts from FE teachers' journals.

Task

- **Read the three following extracts taken from teachers' journals.**

- **Identify those passages you would describe as reflective and those you judge to be simply descriptive.**

- **Decide which of these teachers is providing evidence he or she is learning from his or her professional practice.**

- **Further, specific questions and tasks follow each extract. All the answers will be discussed after the final journal entry.**

EXTRACT ONE
This is from the journal of a full-time student on a PGCE FE course.

> **Monday 11 November**
> My mentor said this morning's lesson was okay. The content was good and that all I need to do is to slow down a bit when I'm talking – and I agree with that.
>
> I'm not sure how nervous I looked, but I felt like the students would be taking more notice of my signs of nervousness than of anything I was saying. I felt I'd planned the content okay, but I'm not sure I made myself understood very well. I did talk too fast, and I didn't put things in a very good order. I need to be surer about what I want to say. And I need to relax a bit instead of trying to drag the lesson along.
>
> I found myself talking to the whiteboard a lot, but then maybe I wouldn't do this if the overheads worked better. I ought to write them in permanent marker next time – or get them typed and photocopied on to the transparency. But I did feel that I got as much response to my questions as [my mentor] usually does. Very difficult to tell whether they're listening, though, or whether they couldn't care less. I suppose at the end of the day there's nothing I can do to make them pay attention or write things down. Next time I might allow more time for them to ask questions.
>
> **Tuesday 12 November**
> I spent hours and hours getting my head round some of the theory last night ready for today's lesson. And I kept thinking, how am I going to be a teacher if I've got to teach the students to get their head round this and I

can't even do that myself? But it's strange really because [my mentor] told me that today's lesson is the best one I've done so far. And then I made the connection. Because by having to spend so much time struggling to learn something, I ended up in a better position to teach it because I knew the bits that caused difficulty, and I wouldn't assume any prior knowledge, so I wouldn't leave anything out. Actually, in terms of planning, I'd thought it would take a lot longer to teach this than it did, and I had time at the end of the lesson to go over it and ask questions.

All in all I think it was a success, and I feel really good about it. This is what I've heard some of the others describing – that you leave the lesson feeling a real buzz.

Wednesday 13 November

This is really strange. Taught the same thing to the other parallel group and it felt totally different. Yesterday's group are much more up for discussion, and were happy to take notes from the overheads, even though it took a long time. Today's group don't show the slightest interest in involving themselves in the lesson and are really slow and reluctant about taking notes from the OHP. Moaned every time a new one went up. The girl who usually gives me grief was worse than usual – never stopped – sighing and putting her head in her hands and all that sort of thing. But I've found that the best way to deal with this is to ignore her. She wants attention, I think, and maybe she'll just get bored and give up trying if I don't give her any. She's not malicious, really, so I don't think ignoring her would make it escalate.

But it's really weird how yesterday's group can focus and today's can't, even though it's the same lesson done in the same way.

Thursday 14 November

I'm going to have to be a bit more assertive. I'm going to have to tell [the reluctant group] to do things, rather than ask nicely, otherwise they're going to keep taking advantage. I think they need to know where the boundaries are and I ought to tell them outright, rather than leaving it to them to test them all the time. They're too used to being given leeway. I'm not sure I'm skilled or confident enough yet, though, to take a different line. Some of them just aren't learning. I give them plenty of opportunities to ask questions, and I go over the stuff several times, and so if they aren't taking the opportunity to learn I don't see there's a lot else I can do.

Close focus

Two additional points you might like to consider about this extract are:

- *What questions would you want to prompt this teacher to ask him or herself?*

- *Identify two points this teacher intends to incorporate into his or her action plan.*

EXTRACT TWO

This is from the journal of a full-time lecturer who has been teaching for just over a year.

> 2/2
> Am getting very stressed about the Advanced class. Seems like there's been no attempt to try and run this module correctly and there's no support and I'm finding it more and more difficult to find new material and assessment methods. I'm losing confidence about taking the class at all, and there's no support. Every time I approach [the section head] he doesn't seem to have any real advice (though he's always friendly). He just seems to leave it to me so I'm back at square one.
>
> There never seems to be an end to it. You finish one class and you're worrying about the next and planning for the next. Though if I'm honest I have got some really good classes and a nice rapport with some of the students. It does help when you're all on the same side. I'm glad I've got the insight to sum people up fairly accurately and quite quickly. It lets me feel my way around how best to present things to the class. The Level Two group were brilliant today. Asked lots of questions and responded really well. I like it that I can make it seem easy.
>
> 8/2
> Got into class this morning and only one student there! Another rolled in about 20 mins late. Should've been 15. I'm going to concentrate on disciplining the ones that miss lessons or turn up late. It's no good them being nice and treating me like a friend and then doing this. I had to change my plan when there were only two of them, so all that time spent planning was wasted. I just made them sit in silence and do their assignment. Then afterwards, when I saw [the section head] and told him, all he said was that the assignment should have been a report and not an essay. This wasn't explained before. It's the old familiar problem – I only find out afterwards when I've done something wrong. No support. And I'm also fed up about the register never being available – somebody not putting it back where it should be. And I know who. So it means I'm not keeping a proper record. I meant to ask [section head] about internal

verification and also about me seeing the External Verifier, but he's always rushing away and I didn't get a chance.

Close focus

1. *Take one of the incidents or experiences from this teacher's journal and rewrite it as a reflective rather than descriptive entry.*

2. *If you were this teacher, what questions would you be asking in your journal?*

3. *What plans of action would you be setting down?*

EXTRACT THREE

This is from the journal of an experienced teacher.

Monday

Took the Advanced students on their trip on Friday as planned. Briefing them several times beforehand seemed to work well, and the work sheets kept them busy on the coach, so that although they were exchanging answers and doing lots of talking they were most of them on task for most of the time. I'll certainly use this strategy another time.

They were pretty well behaved when we got off the coach – just a bit noisy, but I think that's to be expected. They calmed down as requested when we got into the building, and everything was going well until the guide took us up the tower. The spiral staircase is very dark – the windows are spaced at long intervals and they're only arrow slits really, so it's very dark. And it's narrow as well. And the steps narrow to nothing at the inside edge, so you have keep close to the outside wall to find a broad enough tread to get your whole foot on. The guide was at the front, and then about fifteen students, and then me in the middle and Malc at the back behind the other fifteen. I was feeling a bit hemmed in and not very comfortable. We'd been climbing for probably about five minutes when one of Malc's students, about three behind me, started panicking. He was trying to turn round and go down and he was thrashing about and shouting that he had to get out. He was setting some of the others off and there was some squeaking and screaming. I had to let three students go past me before I could get to him, and that meant balancing right on the inside where the step was narrowest so that they could get past safely on the wide bit. Scary! But I couldn't show it. I got down to this lad and tried to calm him down, but he was hysterical, flapping about all over the place. I decided the best thing was to get the others safely past us so that I could take him back down to the bottom. I pulled him to the inside so they could get past and I stood a couple of steps below him, holding him up so he didn't feel as though he could fall off the narrow bit of step, and I told him if he held on for a couple of minutes while they all got past, I'd take him back down. When Malc got up to us, he offered to do it, so I let him because the lad knew him, and I went on with the others, because one of us had to.

What a drama. And now that poor lad's got to live it down. So what have I learnt from this about planning visits?

1) Think ahead to what we'll be doing and identify anything likely to trigger phobias like this.

2) Tell them again, before we do whatever it is – like climbing the tower – that if anyone would rather not, that's OK because one of us teachers will be staying at the bottom (or wherever) anyway to give them an alternative activity.

3) Take an extra member of staff so that we can do this. And make sure at least one of us is a First Aider.

4) Put something in the letter and permission slip we send to parents/carers explaining the proposed activities in detail and asking whether there's any problem. And make sure the insurance covers us for incidents like this.

Otherwise it was all OK and they got lots of stuff for their assignment and seem quite fired up about it.

Close focus

Does this qualify as a reflective piece of writing? If so, why? If not, why not?

Discussion of the three journal extracts

Let's look at the three extracts in terms of the general questions posed at the beginning. You were asked to pick out the reflective passages from the purely descriptive ones and to identify the journal writers who provide evidence they are learning from their professional practice.

EXTRACT ONE

There are three entries from the first journal. The first one, dated 11 November, begins with a flurry of self-criticism. You could call it 'reflective' in the sense it's going over what happened in a critical way, but it's not particularly useful or productive. It's a record of the teacher's self-doubts rather than a measured reflection and plan of action arising from what went well and what did not.

By the third paragraph, however, the writing has become more analytical. It begins to follow a structure that is a basic model for reflection on practice and goes something like this:

- What problems were there with the lesson? ('*I found myself talking to the whiteboard a lot.*')

- Why did they arise? ('... *but then maybe I wouldn't do this if the overheads worked better.*')

- How can I avoid it happening like that next time? ('*I ought to write them in permanent marker next time – or get them typed and photocopied on to the transparency.*')

The fourth paragraph is reflective because it records a real insight into what it was about the teacher's preparation and planning that had made the difficult content of the lesson so accessible to the students. The teacher is focusing on a success here rather than a problem and so, although the written reflection follows the same basic structure, this time the questions have a positive emphasis:

- What succeeded? ('*But it's strange really because [my mentor] told me that today's lesson is the best one I've done so far.*')

- Why? ('*And then I made the connection. Because by having to spend so much time struggling to learn something, I ended up in a better position to teach it because I knew the bits that caused difficulty.*')

- How can I increase the chances of repeating this success? ('... *and I wouldn't assume any prior knowledge, so I wouldn't leave anything out.*')

The fifth and last paragraph for 11 November is in direct contrast to the first. By moving beyond the simple record of self-doubts, the teacher has found that, on reflection, a lot has been learnt from the lesson and there is much to say about it that is positive.

The entry for 13 November provides a comparison of two groups which is largely descriptive. It identifies a problem, certainly; but it doesn't yet pursue a solution. The entry becomes reflective, however, when it turns to the troublesome student. It's reflective because it sets out what the teacher intends to do to remedy the situation and gives the reasons for trying this particular strategy. Again, it follows the familiar structure:

- What succeeded? ('*But I've found that the best way to deal with this is to ignore her.*')

- Why? ('*She wants attention, I think.*')

- How can I increase the chances of repeating this success? ('... *and maybe she'll just get bored and give up trying if I don't give her any.*')

On 14 November the teacher picks up again the problem of the reluctant student group, simply described in the previous entry, and now begins to reflect on what to do about it. The order of the questions is slightly different but the elements of the reflective structure are all there. On Wednesday 13th it only gets as far as: what problems were there with the lesson? ('*One group of students seems reluctant and undermotivated.*') But on Thursday 14th we find the teacher is now considering a solution: how can I avoid it happening like that next time? ('*Be more assertive.*') And finally hypothesising about the cause of the problem: why did the problem arise? ('*The students are too used to being given leeway.*')

There is clear evidence in the extracts from Journal One, therefore, that this teacher is learning from his or her professional practice. You may not agree with all the analyses or solutions this journal-keeper comes up with but, nevertheless, his or her journal is evidence he or she is a reflective practitioner. And so, having read his or her entries and reflected on them yourself, are there any questions you feel this teacher has left unasked? Consider, for example, this sentence from the final paragraph of the entry for Monday 11th:

> 'I suppose at the end of the day there's nothing I can do to **make** them pay attention or write things down.'

Could this be phrased in a more useful way? How far do you think the teacher's resolve – to allow more time for questions – might go towards solving the problem?

EXTRACT TWO

As you will probably have identified at first reading, this teacher's journal entries are very largely descriptive. In his or her first entry there is a brief reflection on how a difficult topic can be made accessible to students by relating it to something within their experience. Useful as this is, however, it appears to be something the teacher has realised already rather than an insight gained by current reflections. In the second entry the teacher resolves to 'discipline' late-comers and non-attenders. Again, this is reflective in the sense it is taking a problem and planning a strategy which may solve it. On the whole, however, this teacher appears to be using the journal more as a diary in which to record frustrations and let off a little steam than as a method for reflecting upon practice and learning from it. The pattern of reflection is absent. Instead, the predominant structure in this extract seems to be:

- What happened?

- How do I feel about it?

The difficulties encountered are mostly attributed to the fault of others and, while this may well be an accurate assessment, there is little or no questioning of the teacher's own practice or consideration of alternative courses of action that might be taken. The extract, therefore, provides little evidence this teacher is a reflective practitioner.

So, if you were this teacher, what questions would you be asking in your journal? (You'll find some ideas in the next section of this chapter.)

EXTRACT THREE

At first it seems this extract is purely descriptive. It relates a dramatic event in quite some detail, and is rather like reading a story. It is not until we come to the action plan at the end that we see this is a useful piece of reflective journal-writing. The teacher records what happened and then answers the key questions: what have I learnt from this? And, what will I do differently next time? There's no agonising internal dialogue here – perhaps I shouldn't have done such-and-such. Such agonising is not an essential part of reflection. In fact, the structure used here is simply an abbreviated version of our familiar model:

- What happened? (The events described in the first two paragraphs.)

- How can I avoid it happening like that next time? (The plan of action that follows.)

The middle step – Why did it happen? – is implicit in the clear and detailed action plan at the end. This teacher, like the first, is providing evidence in the journal of reflective practice.

What sort of things should I include in a reflective journal?

This will very much depend upon what you yourself consider to be critical incidents – incidents and experiences from which there is something to learn. We've seen some examples already in the opening paragraphs of this chapter and in the journal extracts. A careful look at some of the FENTO Standards related to reflection (listed at the beginning of this chapter) will also give you some useful pointers towards the sort of issues you could usefully reflect upon. For example, Skill G3a is common to all three stages and suggests that, as teachers, we should identify where [our] own knowledge and skills need to be updated. Whatever prompts us to do this – whether it is the realisation in planning a lesson that our knowledge of the topic is not sufficiently recent, or whether we find we are not entirely confident about using presentation techniques such as PowerPoint – those experiences and insights are ideal material for the journal, together with a clear reminder to ourselves of what we are going to do about it. One of your aims, if you are following a FENTO-endorsed programme, will be to cover at least those areas indicated in the standards as being appropriate to your stage of the qualification. You will find the lists at the beginning of this chapter a useful guide for identifying those areas of your professional practice that could receive particular attention in your journal. If, for example, you realise on reading through your journal that you have never recorded your thoughts about the way in which the results of student assessment have caused you to revise or rethink aspects of your teaching (F2d), you may choose to make this the focus of your next journal entry.

Your conclusion might justifiably be that poor assessment results were nothing at all to do with the quality of the teaching. On the other hand you might, on reflection, conclude the students needed to be more actively involved in their learning or needed some help with their note-taking skills. You may then try out this solution when next planning for a similar group or topic. If it doesn't work, you can record this in your journal, reflect again and perhaps try another solution.

Some of you will recognise this process of action, reflection, revised action, reflection, as a simplified model of educational action research. In a sense, when you keep a reflective journal about your professional practice, this is what you are engaged in. You are asking yourself, among others, the following questions:

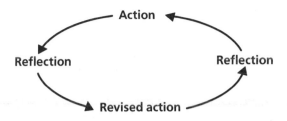

A simplified model of educational action research

- What happened?
- What would I like to change, and why?
- What action could I realistically take to change it?
- Did it work?
- If so, is there a general principle here I can use again?
- If not, what could I try next, and why?

As long as you get beyond that first question, you are on your way to being a reflective practitioner.

Here are some further questions you might like to use to ensure your journal moves beyond the purely descriptive. They are intended as a guide only. As you become used to keeping a journal and discover its benefits, you'll find you don't need a checklist to help you to write reflectively.

✓ Why am I choosing to write about this particular incident or experience?

✓ How do I feel about it?

✓ What have I learnt from it about:

- myself;
- my subject knowledge;
- my professional skills;
- my students?

✓ What were the successes involved? What could I learn from it in order to do it again?

✓ If there was a problem, was it within my control to prevent it?

✓ If it was within my control, what could I have done differently?

✓ When might there be a practical opportunity to see whether this different strategy works better?

✓ If it wasn't within my control, are there nevertheless any measures I can take now to reduce the possibility of this happening again?

✓ Has this shown any gaps in my professional practice or subject knowledge?

✓ If so, how will I go about filling them?

✓ Did I enjoy teaching this lesson? If so, why? If not, why not?

✓ Did the students seem to enjoy their experience of learning? If so, why? If not, why not? If I don't know, how could I find out next time?

✓ Were the learning outcomes achieved? How do I know? If not, what can I change in order to make it more likely they are achieved next time? If I don't know, how can I revise my lesson plans to make sure I have this information?

✓ If I am writing about a lesson I participated in as a learner rather than as a teacher, what have I learnt in terms of dos and don'ts that will be useful for my own professional practice?

How much should I write, and how often?

Again, this will depend very much upon your circumstances. The key words here are 'ongoing' and 'sufficient'. If you are a part-time teacher at the Introduction stage, the range and number of your teaching experiences will be more limited than at the Intermediate or Certification stages, for example. The important thing is that you should not think of the journal as simply a hoop you are being asked to jump through. It's a useful tool for any teacher, particularly those who are actively involved in professional development – and ideally that should mean all of us. It would be a pity, therefore, to see the journal as a chore or as a purely instrumental step towards gaining your FENTO-endorsed qualification. You may not write in it every day – indeed, it would be remarkable if you had the time to – but you should aim at first to make at least one journal entry each week in which you record and reflect upon an aspect of your practice, an incident or experience that has occupied your mind. In an incident-filled week you may make several journal entries.

The number of words you write isn't crucial. What is important is that the emphasis is upon reflection rather than description. If you are asking yourself questions and attempting to answer them, this is an indication you are being reflective. As we saw from the journal extracts earlier in this chapter, some people's reflections can be quite succinct while others find it useful to 'think aloud' and express themselves at great length. It isn't the quantity but the reflective quality that counts.

If the process of reflection has been productive, it will usually end in an action point or an entire plan of action. In this sense your journal becomes an ongoing and discursive action plan, charting your concerns, your solutions, your professional needs and your successes. In other words, you are charting and planning your own professional development.

What if I'm a student teacher with no prior classroom experience to record?

First of all it has to be said that you almost certainly do have classroom experience – as a learner. And as learners we are constantly reflecting on how we are being taught (whether we do this consciously or not) and identifying which teachers or teaching styles or activities we learn from best, and why. Although the standards require you to reflect upon your own practice, your experiences as a learner can be a useful starting point for this. As a full-time student teacher on an initial PGCE or Cert Ed programme, you will very quickly find yourself being given opportunities to teach, whether it is micro-teaching exercises to the rest of your group or under guidance at the college that hosts your teaching practice. Initially, you will be in a similar position to that of a teacher at the FENTO Introduction stage, having a limited range of teaching experiences to draw upon. Like them, you need to remember that 'stage', in the sense that FENTO intends it, is not synonymous with level, and that you will therefore be expected to demonstrate the same capacity for reflection as a full-time teacher. The experiences you have to draw upon will be fewer and more limited in scope, but your depth of reflection and your ability to learn and plan from these experiences should be unaffected by this.

So, let's assume you are at the beginning of your initial teacher education and that so far you have only your experiences as a learner to reflect upon. Taking these as your starting point, here are some questions you could usefully explore in your journal pages.

Who would I identify as the best teacher I ever had, and why?
This might be Ms Plumpton at primary school, who showed a special interest in your artwork; or a college lecturer who made you realise for the first time that learning could be fun. When you've decided whom to nominate as your best teacher, write down a list of the qualities that made him or her so. It needn't be a very long list – two or three sentences would do – but take some time to think about it.

Now look at what you've written. The chances are the qualities you admired in your best teacher will be ones you are hoping to develop yourself. In other words, consciously or not, it's likely that, to some extent, you will take your best teacher as a role model or benchmark for your own classroom practice. If your best teacher was impressively authoritative about his or her subject, this is one of the main standards you'll measure your own success by. If he or she was a stern disciplinarian, you'll be drawing on his or her strategies for keeping order. Perhaps the qualities you identified in your best teacher were his or her enthusiasm for his or her subject and his or her ability to make students or pupils feel he or she cared about their learning. If this is so, it's no surprise. These are the qualities the majority of people associate with their best teacher. And that in itself is worth reflecting on.

Another question you could explore is: what am I most looking forward to about teaching, and what aspect, if any, is worrying me?
This will help you to identify what you perceive as your current strengths and weaknesses and will allow you to draft out a preliminary action plan. As you begin to gain some practical classroom experience as a teacher, you can refer back to this starting point to reflect upon how your perception of your strengths and weaknesses is changing, and to consider how new priorities might cause you to revise your plan of action.

You might also like to ask yourself: what do my current experiences as a learner tell me about what to do and what not to do when it's my turn to be up there teaching?
You can identify the teaching styles, the learning activities, the methods and strategies you would like to add to your own repertoire. You can observe and record the reactions of other student teachers in your group and consider why some will respond well to certain teaching styles and learning activities which you yourself may have found less enjoyable. You can observe your tutors making the occasional mistake and reflect that it isn't necessary always to be perfect. You'll relax and enjoy your teaching so much more if you keep this in mind. And if you're enjoying your teaching, that's usually a good indication that your students are, too.

How can my journal be used as evidence I'm meeting the FENTO Standards?

Your journal is an important source of evidence that you are reflecting on your practice. Remember, you do not have to link every entry in an instrumental way to the FENTO Standards. The standards are there to provide guidance to direct you to the sort of issues you should be reflecting on, and for what purpose. When the time comes to submit coursework or evidence from your professional practice in order for you to achieve your qualification, your journal can be submitted in fulfilment, or partial fulfilment, of the requirements for reflective practice.

If there are entries in your journal you would rather not share – if, for example, you have been confiding some of your darker moods or frustrations or have mentioned people by name in an uncomplimentary light – you may wish to edit your journal before submitting it, or to submit only extracts. If you are of a very orderly frame of mind or if you feel it might be of help to your assessor or external examiner, you may like to highlight some of the reflective passages which best illustrate the key steps in your professional development. You may even wish to cross-reference some of your reflections to the standards, although this is not strictly necessary.

Other evidence of research and reflection

The journal will probably not be the only source of evidence that you are a reflective practitioner, although it is likely to be the main one. You may be required, as part of your college's self-assessment strategy, to prepare your own written evaluation of those of your lessons which are observed for quality assurance purposes. If you are a student teacher, you will be expected to produce evaluations of the lessons you teach on teaching practice, and these may be required separately from your journal. (For guidance on lesson evaluations, see Chapters 3 and 7.)

And the Key Skills?

As a form of written communication (even though it's addressed primarily to yourself), the reflective journal is an opportunity to demonstrate you are meeting some of the Level 3 Key Skill requirements in Communication. If you are keeping your journal electronically, you will be demonstrating some of the Level 2 Key Skills in IT (including, it's very much to be hoped, always remembering to keep a backup copy!).

Further reading

Bolton, G. (2001) *Reflective Practice: Writing and Professional Development.* London: Paul Chapman.

Carr, W. and Kemmis, S. (1986) *Becoming Critical: Education, Knowledge and Action Research.* London: Falmer Press.

Handal, G. and Lauvas, P. (1987) *Promoting Reflective Teaching.* Milton Keynes: Open University Press.

Hollingworth, S. (ed.) (1997) *International Action Research.* London: Falmer Press.

Moon, J. A. (1999) *Reflection in Learning and Professional Development: Theory and Practice.* London: Kogan Page.

3 PLANNING AND PREPARING TEACHING AND LEARNING PROGRAMMES FOR GROUPS AND INDIVIDUALS

This chapter examines useful ways to plan and prepare and it discusses the advantages to the teacher of careful, formalised planning. It also explains how such documentation of your planning can be used to demonstrate you are meeting the related standards in terms of knowledge and the skills appropriate to your stage. The ideas and advice in this chapter relate mainly to the following areas of skills and knowledge.

→ **Introduction stage**
   Skills: B1a, B1c, B1d, B2a, B2e, B3b, B3d

→ **Intermediate stage. All the above, plus**
   Skills: B1b, B1e, B2b, B2c, B2f, B3c, B3d, B3e

→ **Certification stage. All the above, plus**
   Skills: B1f, B2d, B3a, B3f, B3g, B3h

→ **Essential knowledge**
   A range of essential knowledge that includes areas listed under b1, b2, b3

You may find the tasks and discussion in this chapter lead you to undertake activities or to produce materials that demonstrate skills and knowledge relevant to other key areas. The listings above shouldn't, therefore, be taken as exhaustive.

Why plan?

When student teachers return after their first visit to a college, one or two of them always tells the same story. They have asked an experienced member of staff for tips on lesson planning or for permission to look at his or her plan for a particular lesson, only to be told: 'Oh, there's no time for that, not in the *real* world. You just keep it in here.' And the experienced teacher has tapped his or her head and smiled. And the student teacher, left holding forlornly on to his or her own carefully drawn A4 lesson plan, wonders whether his or her PGCE course is offering duff advice.

Not so. The process of constructing a visible lesson plan is not simply an instrumental exercise; it has an equally important developmental function. In other words, its purpose is not only to plot the course of the lesson. The very process of drawing up the plan encourages the teacher to reflect on how and why the content is chosen and sequenced and best presented. It also remains useful well beyond the end of the lesson. As a record of intention, it allows the teacher to review and reflect upon what went to plan, what did not and why. It provides the teacher with a record of teaching and learning strategies from which to identify which ones the students respond to best and whether any are being over- or under-used. It allows the teacher to check whether assessment strategies have been incorporated to monitor the achievement of each planned outcome. And much, much more – as we shall see. A lesson plan that is formulated only in the head and remains there does not help facilitate any of these activities, all of which are central to good professional practice. The time saved in not committing a lesson plan to disk or to paper is a false economy. It's likely to result in time being spent later looking for assessment evidence or for gaps in the coverage of the course specifications; or time wasted on teaching and learning strategies to which students have already shown themselves to be unresponsive. There is, of course, an instrumental argument, too, for producing lesson plans on paper (or at least on disk) in that they are needed to satisfy the requirements of Ofsted, the Adult Learning Inspectorate (ALI) and the college's own self-assessment programme. But these requirements simply reflect the key issue that documented planning is, in itself, both a function and a measure of reflective professional development.

To plan at all, however, we first need to know where we are going. We need a clearly articulated target; a target that is sufficiently clearly stated that we will be in no doubt as to whether we have achieved it. In lesson planning we refer to our targets as learning outcomes or objectives. Sometimes these are stated for us in the course specifications or syllabus. If we are involved with the teaching, learning and assessment of students or trainees working towards a competence-based award such as an NVQ, the targets will be stated for us in terms of the performance criteria the students must meet. The learning outcomes for your lesson plan must be clear and they must be observable in some way in order for you to know whether learning has actually taken place.

Task

Consider the following topics which students might be expected to learn, and decide how you would know, by the end of the lesson or series of lessons, whether the learning had been successful:

- *tying a reef knot;*

- *knowing why Napoleon was exiled to St Helena;*

- *understanding the factors involved in social exclusion;*

- *the difference between a theme park and a tourist attraction;*

- *not to allow contamination between cooked and uncooked meats.*

TYING A REEF KNOT
The only way you'd know whether the students had learnt this successfully would be to see them do it. Your target, or learning outcome, therefore, would be: 'By the end of the lesson the students will be able to tie a reef knot.' And so within the

planned lesson you would have to provide opportunities for them to practise this and to demonstrate their learning. How many times would you want to see a student tie the knot correctly before you assessed him or her as having correctly achieved the outcome?

KNOWING WHY NAPOLEON WAS EXILED TO ST HELENA

The big question here is, how will you know whether students know this by the end of the lesson? You will know whether you've explained it to them, but it doesn't necessarily follow they've understood. You can't see whether they know it in the same way you can see whether they can tie a reef knot. 'Know' is not, therefore a very useful word when constructing outcomes. So what would constitute reliable evidence that students did know why Napoleon was exiled to St Helena? Well, they could list the reasons or they could explain the reasons. They might do this during questions and answers in class or as part of a written assignment, or both. Your outcome will then be: 'By the end of the lesson the students will be able to explain [or list the reasons] why Napoleon was exiled to St Helena.' Only if they list or explain will you be able to ascertain reliably whether they know.

UNDERSTAND THE FACTORS INVOLVED IN SOCIAL EXCLUSION

This sounds like an outcome, but it's of very little use to you if you're looking for evidence learning has taken place. Unless your students live in a comic strip, there'll be no light bulb suddenly appearing above their heads to indicate they've understood. 'Understand' is no more observable than 'know'. They simply aren't useful terms when constructing learning outcomes. Here again, 'list' and 'explain' serve our purpose far better. They will provide observable evidence of whether or not learning has taken place. But remember, if you are to know whether by the end of the lesson the students will be able to list the factors involved in social exclusion, you must include in your lesson plan some student activity or activities that will enable you to assess whether they can in fact list these factors correctly.

THE DIFFERENCE BETWEEN A THEME PARK AND A TOURIST ATTRACTION

Again, 'know' and 'understand' won't help us with our planning but 'list' or 'explain the differences' will.

NOT TO ALLOW CONTAMINATION BETWEEN COOKED AND UNCOOKED MEATS

This is an interesting one because it is about good practice and is therefore an aspect of their learning students should always be seen to demonstrate when the context demands it. It isn't enough they know it should be done and can explain why. They must be seen to do it. The outcome, therefore, needs to be very specific. The student will avoid contamination between cooked and uncooked meats by always storing and displaying the two separately, and never handling them with the same implements. Compare this with the reef knot. How many times would you need to assess students on this outcome before you were satisfied it had been achieved?

Having argued for documented lesson planning and for clearly stated, observable outcomes, the next questions are: what should be included in the plan, and what is the most useful format to use? To consider these, let's have a look at the two lesson plans below.

Task

Read through these two versions of a plan for the same lesson, in conjunction with the handout the teacher has prepared:

- **Which version of the lesson plan would be more useful to the teacher during the planning stage, and why?**

- **Which would be more useful to the teacher during the lesson itself, and why?**

- **Which would be more useful for the purposes of evaluation and reflection after the lesson, and why?**

LESSON PLAN

Date:

Subject/level: Business Advanced; Year 1; No. of students: 15

Duration: 45 mins.

Topic: Preparing presentations.

Aims: To encourage the students to think about the elements that go into making a good presentation.

  To make the topic enjoyable and interesting by 'auctioning' these elements, one by one, to the highest bidder.

Outcomes: Students will be able to: 1) List the key elements that go into giving a good presentation; 2) identify those they consider most important; 3) explain and justify their choice; 4) draw up an appropriate plan of action, with rationale, in preparation for their next presentation.

Content:

1) Introduce topic (3 mins)

2) Students brainstorm key elements; teacher lists them on board

3) Auction sheets. Each student decides how much to bid for what

4) Hold auction

5) Whole group discussion about individual and group priorities

6) Individual work on action plans.

Methods: Brainstorming; game; whole-group discussion.

Assessment: Individual and group responses. Completed action plans and rationales.

Resources: Whiteboard, pens, auction sheet handouts.

Key Skill opportunities: Calculating sums to bid (A of N); group discussion and written plan (Communication).

Lesson plan version A

Time	Content	Outcomes	Method	Student Activity	Assessment	Key Skills	Resources
10.30	Introduce topic		Exposition	Listen, ask questions		Listening (Com)	
10.33	Elements of a good presentation	List elements of a good presentation	Brainstorm	Students brainstorm elements	Observe Individual responses		Whiteboard and pens
10.38	Teacher explains auction		Exposition	Listen, ask questions, plan bids		Calculating bids	Auction sheets (handouts)
10.42	Hold auction	Identify elements they consider most important	Game/ simulation	Bid for elements they've chosen	Observe and record bidding		
10.52	Discuss individual and group priorities	Explain and justify their choice	Whole group discussion	Listen and contribute to discussion	Observe individual responses	Discussion (Com)	
11.00	Individual action plans	Draw up an individual action plan for preparing and making a presentation	Individual practical work	Apply what they've learnt to drawing up their action plans	Assess action plans		

Aims: To encourage the students to think about the elements that go into making a good presentation.
To make the topic enjoyable and interesting by 'auctioning' each element to the highest bidder.

Date: _____ Subject/level: Business Advanced Y1. Duration: 45 mins. No of students: 15

Lesson plan version B

The Presentation Skills Auction

You have £2000 with which to bid for the skills and qualities you think would be most useful in making a clear and interesting presentation.

All the skills and qualities listed below will be auctioned to the highest bidder. Decide what you want to bid for, and write the figure for the highest bid you are prepared to make in the 'Amount I will bid' column. The total of this column should not come to more than £2000.

If you fail in a bid, you cannot use the sum you allocated to bid for anything else.

As the auction proceeds, write down in the right-hand column the winning bid against each item.

Useful skills and qualities for presentation	Amount I will bid	Winning Bid
Careful planning		
Clear voice		
Well-produced visual aids		
Good sense of humour		
Ability to speak without notes		
Smartly dressed		
Logical sequencing of material		
Using a vocabulary the audience understands		
A pleasant, informal approach		
Leaving time for questions at the end		

Presentation skills auction: revised handout

There is something to be said for both these lesson plan formats. The first may seem more immediately accessible in terms of 'telling the story' of the lesson. There's less need for abbreviation and we may feel more comfortable with this familiar, discursive form. The second looks as though it may be more time-consuming to prepare and, if we haven't written it ourselves, we have to work harder initially to follow what's happening in the lesson. But if we look at our first question ('Which version of the lesson plan would be more useful to the teacher during the planning stage, and why?') the answer would almost certainly be version B, for the following reasons.

Its systematic layout, using rows and columns, makes it more difficult for the teacher to overlook any aspect necessary to the planning process. For example, following the rows against each objective/outcome, the teacher can see clearly whether the planned student activity is designed to bring that outcome about and whether an appropriate and realistic assessment activity is in place to monitor whether the outcome has been achieved. And following the rows under 'Method' and 'Student activity', the teacher can check at a glance whether the plan has allowed for the students to become actively engaged in their learning and whether it provides sufficient variety of activity to stimulate and maintain their interest. This format also allows the teacher to plot exactly where the activities of the lesson will create natural opportunities for the development of Key Skills. Version B is therefore a useful instrument in the planning and preparation of the lesson. It is helpful to the process and is, in this sense, developmental.

Our second question asked: which would be more useful to the teacher during the lesson itself, and why? Here again, version B has some clear advantages:

- the two left-hand columns ('Time' and 'Content') allow the teacher to see at a glance what should be happening now, and what happens next;

- the 'Assessment' column reminds the teacher what he or she should be looking for at each stage of the lesson in terms of evidence of achievement;

- it shows at a glance the exact points in the lesson where the students should be reminded of the opportunities to develop and demonstrate Key Skills;

- the 'Student activity' column summarises what the students should be doing at any given time if they are on task.

Our third question was: which would be more useful for the purposes of evaluation and reflection after the lesson, and why? Again, it seems clear the format most accessible to analysis is version B. The questions the teacher is likely to reflect on after the lesson — such as why the outcomes were or were not achieved; how enthusiastically the students engaged with their learning; whether the pacing of the various stages worked in practice; and so on — can be reviewed more easily from this version of the plan. This is because it charts clearly the relationship of outcomes to activities (and of both these to assessment), and it also clearly displays the sequence and duration of the various activities.

Perhaps the greatest advantage of version B is that it reveals at a glance whether the key formula for effective lesson planning is in place. That is, whether for each objective or outcome there is an opportunity for the students to practise and demonstrate achievement of that outcome, and an assessment method or instrument to measure and record that achievement. The rows and columns of version B make it easier for the teacher to check this formula is in place than does the more discursive format of version A.

Time	Contents	Outcomes	Method	Student activity	Assessment	Key Skills	Resources
What happens next?		What students will be able to do by the end of the lesson	How they will learn to do it	How you will see them doing it.	How you will check whether they can do it	What Key Skills they will be able to demonstrate in the process	What resources you will need to support this learning

Version B: rows and columns format

If you felt version A has clear advantages that aren't mentioned here, you may wish to debate this with your mentor or colleagues. It is also an ideal question to reflect on in your journal, having first tried putting each of the versions into practice.

The lesson plan as evidence of standards-based practice

The lesson plan in chart form has another advantage. It allows us more easily to carry out an audit of our planning skills against those listed in the standards and also to identify where our lesson planning is providing evidence of meeting skills from other key areas.

Close focus

Look at version B of the lesson plan again to see if you can identify the features or components that relate to the following FENTO skills:

- *B1b: 'Produce learning outcomes from programmes of study'*

- *B1c: 'Establish precise learning objectives and content'*

- *B1d: 'Define the subject knowledge, technical knowledge and skills required'*

- *B1f: ' Key Skills are integral to provision as required'*

- *B2f: 'Encourage learners to see the relevance of what they are learning to other aspects of the curriculum'*

- *B2a, B2b, B2c, C2e: 'Encourage learners to adopt styles of learning appropriate to the outcomes and to their own needs as individuals and as a group'*

- *C1d: 'Produce interesting and appropriate materials'*

- *C2h: 'Make best use of available resources'*

- *F1e: 'Plan realistic and relevant assessment activities that encourage learning as well as assessing specified outcomes'*

There is evidence from this lesson plan that the teacher's practice, here at least, is consistent with all those skills. The evidence can be found in the plan as follows:

- B1b, B1c, B1d: the 'Outcomes' and 'Content' columns;

- B1f, B2f: the 'Key Skills' column;

- B2a, B2b, B2c, C2e: the 'Methods' and 'Student activity' columns';

- C1d, C2h: the 'Resources' column;

- Fle: the 'Assessment' column.

Time	Contents	Outcomes	Method	Student activity	Assessment	Key Skills	Resources
	B1b, B1c, B1d	B1b, B1c, B1d	B2a, B2b, B2c, C2e	B2a, B2b, B2c, C2e	F1e	B1f, B2f	C1d, C2h

Version B: evidence

Close focus

There are other aspects of the lesson plan which suggest the teacher is practising in conformity with the standards. Out of professional interest, and to familiarise yourself further with the standards, you may like to refer to the skills listed in the Appendix to identify more of these.

Reflective planning

We discussed earlier some of the ways in which a clearly drawn-up lesson plan can be helpful during the process of reflection when the lesson is over; now we're going to explore that process a little further. Having seen the teacher's lesson plan, let's look at the teacher's own journal account of how that lesson worked out in practice.

Task

Read through the journal pages that follow and consider these questions:

- *How would you distinguish between the purpose of the first and second paragraphs?*

- *What aspects of the planning does the teacher identify as needing some revision?*

October 22

Had the 1st year Advanced Business this morning. They've got to do their first assessed presentations in two weeks and they've been making a great fuss about it – about being too nervous and all the rest of it. The problem I have with this group is that they never seem very motivated to do anything. I don't think I've ever seen a flicker of enthusiasm from them about anything, and it seems a shame, because they're a bright lot on the whole, and a nice bunch. So I've been casting around for some ideas to make the sessions really interesting, to have a bit of fun and make sure they're all involved. And I hit on this idea of an auction, with me as the auctioneer and them all bidding against each other for the aspects of a good presentation they think are most important. E.g. Careful preparation, time for questions, clear visual aids, and so on. I drew up printed lists of these various aspects with a box against each for them to record how much they were going to allow themselves to bid for that item. They were to have £2000 each, and couldn't let their bids run over that total. So really it was a way of getting them to think and prioritise and (hopefully) realise that no single aspect will ensure a good presentation without the others. The least confident or more artistic ones might otherwise spend all their time producing beautiful overheads, for example, and not put effort into other aspects at all. The discussion following the auction was designed to bring all this out. And then, with all this fresh in their minds, they could begin their individual action plans for the presentations. I'd decided to give Gaz the choice of joining in or, if he didn't want to, to monitor the auction and keep a record of the highest amount bid for each aspect so that we could refer to this in our discussion afterwards. The novelty of the auction, and the fact that it involved everyone in a way that was potentially fun, was supposed to jolt them out of their lethargy and motivate them a bit more. That was the plan.

I think on the whole it worked, at least for some of them. The brainstorm at the outset was a bit of a damp squib because only the usual three or four joined in. So it took longer than I'd bargained for to get a reasonable list up on the board that included most of the aspects I'd got listed on the handout. When I gave out the handout, I found I had to explain several times the rules about allocating their £2000. They wanted to know whether, if their bid failed, they could carry the allocated sum over and add it to another bid. I hadn't thought that one out – hadn't seen it coming. I said no. But on reflection it might have been useful for their App. of No. to do a few sums! As it was, they took for ever to decide themselves what to bid for and to write it down, so that by the time we started the auction proper we were more than half way through the lesson. But the auction went very well. I got into role, encouraging bids, slamming the hammer down. Gaz monitored the bids. The students all got animated and, for the first time, really engaged with what they were learning. The whole-group discussion afterwards worked well, too. I think everyone had something to say, and some of them got quite heated about their own view of what was important in a good presentation. The trouble was, there was hardly any time left for the writing of action plans, and this is a worry because all that energy and enthusiasm may have dissipated by next week and we'll have lost some of the ground gained. I set the action plans as homework, but that's never ideal. It means I can't be monitoring them during the process and prompting them or asking questions. Another problem I see in retrospect is that it was unrealistic to assume I could carry out any useful assessment based on the group activities. If they don't all contribute and there's no clear assessment evidence, such 'snapshot', impressionistic assessment isn't very helpful to anybody. The real assessment evidence will be the action plans, which I'll now have to nag them for. All in all, though, it felt like a moderate success. I got them engaged with their learning and let them see that learning can be enjoyable. I should be able to build on that now.

The two paragraphs in this journal account each serve a different purpose. The first offers a justification or rationale for the way in which the lesson was planned. The second offers an evaluation of how far that plan succeeded in practice. These two stages of analysis are both of great importance to reflective practice. They may be carried out and presented with varying degrees of formality. If you are on a full-time or part-time PGCE or Cert Ed programme, for example, you may be required to present a written rationale and evaluation with your lesson plan each time your teaching is observed and assessed. The same may be true if you are involved in appraisal or in some phases of your college's self-assessment. Or you may set out your rationale and evaluation less formally in your reflective journal. Whatever the degree of formality, the rationale for your planning should be transparent and clearly articulated even if, in the first instance, to yourself only.

So, let's look at our second question now: what aspects of the planning does the teacher identify as needing some revision? Since we've been allowed to read part of his journal, we must know him fairly well. So let's call him Jim. His two main areas of concern are timing and assessment. He has underestimated the length of time needed to elicit ideas from the students about what goes to make a good presentation; the time needed to explain clearly how the auction sheet was to be used; and the time the students would take to decide and calculate their intended bids. Jim has also realised that assessment of individuals during group activities can be difficult and unreliable, and becomes quite impossible when some students do not participate fully in the assessed activity. Now, if Jim has a parallel class to teach, or another class who need to prepare for presentations in the near future and might respond well to this approach, the lesson plan can be revised in the light of these reflections and used again, perhaps with even more success.

Close focus

What advice would you give to Jim about the way the lesson plan could be revised or changed in order to overcome the difficulties of timing and assessment?

The problem of timing is a tricky one. It's difficult to see, in so short a session, how the lesson may be trimmed without losing some essential step in the sequence of learning activities. The only area of flexibility seems to be in the list of qualities that make a good presentation. Perhaps Jim himself could do a little prioritising here and produce a shorter list for the auction. This would cut down on the time needed by the students to decide how to allocate their money, and cut down on the time spent on the auction itself. More time would perhaps then be available to spend on the crucial activity of action planning. It would perhaps be unwise to cut down on time spent on the whole-group discussion, as this is central to the sharing and examination of ideas.

As for the issue of assessment, it may well be that the students' individual action plans will themselves be sufficient assessment evidence that the lesson outcomes have been achieved. As additional evidence, however, the teacher may decide to collect the completed auction sheets, since a comparison between these and the action plans may show some movement of ideas and indicate what individual students have learnt from the discussion.

Planning, preparation and the reflective cycle

The reflective cycle that, as we saw in the previous chapter, is central to the keeping of a journal, applies equally, then, to the process of planning and preparation. It looks something like the following. It follows the model of action–reflection–revised action, which should be central to the teacher's professional practice.

The reflective cycle

What questions should I ask myself in the initial process of planning?

Our reading of Jim's journal extract and lesson plan already provides a number of ideas as to the questions it is useful to ask ourselves. These may include some or all of the questions in the following checklist. There may be many more questions you'll want to add to this checklist from your own experience or from your reading of the following chapters. For the time being, let's take the last question and look at it in more detail.

> ✓ Do the outcomes as I have written them, accurately reflect the requirements of the syllabus or course specifications?
> ✓ Are the outcomes observable, assessable and realistic?
> ✓ How will each outcome be assessed?
> ✓ Are the methods and student activities appropriate to these students?
> ✓ Do the activities provide sufficient variety?
> ✓ Do the students have the skills (e.g. note-taking) to make best use of the learning opportunities?
> ✓ Are the planned activities achievable within the time constraints?
> ✓ Is there sufficient planned material for the time available?
> ✓ Do the planned assessment methods allow for accurate assessment of individuals' achievement?
> ✓ What opportunities are there for the students to develop and demonstrate Key Skills? Is it possible to create more of these opportunities in the lesson?

✓ Are the learning materials (in this case the handout) clear, accessible and useful?

✓ Do the learning materials encourage students to engage with, and to take responsibility for, their learning?

✓ Is anything in the planned lesson likely to create barriers to inclusiveness? How can I ensure the lesson presents no such barriers?

Initial process of planning: checklist

Planning for inclusiveness

Inclusiveness, just as much as reflective practice, is a core value underpinning the FENTO Standards. This is what FENTO (2000) has to say:

'**Entitlement, equality and inclusiveness**
Equality of opportunity is a crucial foundation upon which good teaching, learning and assessment are based. All learners should have access to appropriate educational opportunities regardless of ethnic origin, gender, age, sexual orientation, or degree of learning disability and/or difficulty. Consequently, the values of entitlement, equality, and inclusiveness are of fundamental importance to teachers and teaching teams.'

A key consideration in the planning and preparation of any lesson, therefore, is that it should create learning activities which are accessible to all the students and which do not make any student feel excluded, directly or by implication. Close reading of the journal extract we have just been considering suggests that Jim has been keeping this in mind. Mention is made twice of Gaz – presumably a student – and the plan to offer him an alternative to joining in the auction. The rationale for the lesson includes this:

'I'd decided to give Gaz the choice of joining in or, if he didn't want to, to monitor the auction and keep a record of the highest amount bid for each aspect so that we could refer to this in our discussion afterwards.'

and the evaluation tells us: '*Gaz monitored the bids.*'

We aren't given any clue as to why the teacher decided it was best to give Gaz a choice. Presumably the teacher's concern was that Gaz could experience some genuine difficulty over participating in the auction exercise. Notice that Jim did not take it for granted Gaz would not participate, but that he offered him an alternative and equally relevant learning experience and an essential role in the group exercise.

This strategy does not show up, however, on the lesson plan. We only learn of it when we read the lesson rationale and evaluation in the journal. If Jim wanted to demonstrate his lesson planning was informed by the need for inclusiveness, he would not be able to do this by presenting this lesson plan alone. The evidence would be there in the actual lesson, observed perhaps by a mentor or tutor or appraiser; and it would be in Jim's reflective journal, too, or documented separately in a written rationale. There is a good argument, however, for including such strategies in the written lesson plan. An additional column headed 'Individual needs' would remind the teacher at the planning stage to think carefully about the issue of inclusiveness in relation to the students for whom the learning experiences are being planned. And it would act as a reminder after the lesson to evaluate the success or otherwise of these alternative strategies, which might also have included different ways of assessing or recording an individual's achievement.

In some cases, however, it's more appropriate for a student to have his or her own individual learning plan (ILP). Imagine, for example, you are timetabled to teach basic skills. You have a group of eight students, all of whom are at different stages in their learning and have different needs in terms of your support and input. One might be working on her comprehension and written English by reading an application form and filling it in; while another student might still be at the stage of needing help to read simple sentences. A lesson plan that imposed the same activities on all the students would, in this context, be a nonsense. For each student you will need to produce an individual learning plan, with individual targets or planned outcomes and individual activities. As you move from student to student, giving help, advice and encouragement, you will be able to monitor the activity, progress and achievement of each against his or her individual plan.

More will be said about inclusiveness and reflective practice in the chapters that follow because, as core values, they inform every aspect of our work.

Should I write a formal plan for every lesson?

Despite what some cynical old hands will tell you, the answer to this is 'yes'. Formal planning is not an empty exercise. It allows us to think things through carefully and to make adequate preparations. It directs our attention systematically to the needs of our students and the requirements of their syllabus or course specifications. It encourages us to allocate time productively and sensibly. It acts as a 'prompt' or 'script' of sorts while the lesson is in progress. And it helps us to focus on key issues and concerns when we come to evaluate and reflect. The lesson plan is not just instrumental but developmental as well; and for that reason it is worth every gram of effort we put into it. If you are planning a programme of learning or a scheme of work, you will be producing, in essence, a series of linked lesson plans. And here other factors (such as the sequencing of topics, the pace and the assessment deadlines) become important factors – factors that cannot be easily addressed without careful, formalised planning. So, yes, ideally, plan out each lesson. Not only is it good professional practice but it will also make your life easier in the long run.

The contingency plan

Remember that it's always a good idea to have a backup or contingency plan. This doesn't mean a whole full-blown alternative lesson plan. It means having a strategy up your sleeve in case something doesn't go according to plan. If the students get through the lesson more quickly than you had expected, do you have some additional relevant task or input for them? If there's been some slip-up in communications – and you're met by a chorus of 'We've done this already!' – have you got a strategy for adapting the lesson so it becomes an interesting revision session? If something is taking longer than you planned, do you have a short-cut to the end of the lesson without abandoning any of the objectives? In case the OHP isn't working, having you got a whiteboard marker in your pocket? These are all versions of Plan B; and Plan B should be the only plan you keep entirely in your head!

Other evidence of planning and preparation

Your lesson plans will not be the only evidence of your planning and preparation. There will also be, as we have seen, schemes of work, integrated learning programmes and individual learning plans. Course materials, and resources such as handouts, overhead transparencies and PowerPoint presentations, are all evidence of the care you take over the preparation and planning of lessons. There is likely to be evidence in your journal, too, of course, and in the rationale you produce, either in your journal or separately.

Further reading and useful websites

Reading

Armitage, A. *et al.* (1999) *Teaching and Training in Post-Compulsory Education.* Buckingham: Open University Press (Chap. 8).

Reece, I. and Walker, S. (1994) *A Practical Guide to Teaching, Training and Learning.* Sunderland: Business Education Publishers (Chap. 5).

Walkin, L. (1990) *Teaching and Learning in Further and Adult Education.* Cheltenham: Stanley Thornes (Chap. 4).

Website

The Qualifications and Curriculum Authority for Key Skills and other 14–19 curriculum information – www.qca.org.uk

4 ASSESSING LEARNERS' NEEDS AND PROVIDING LEARNERS WITH SUPPORT

This chapter focuses on the importance of making an initial assessment of your students' needs and previous experiences of learning, and on the ways in which you can use this information to find appropriate ways to provide students with the support they need. These issues are illustrated and explored through the use of a case study presented in the form of extracts from a teacher's journal. They relate to the following areas of skills and knowledge.

→ **Introduction stage**
Skills: A1a, A2a, A2h, E1f, E2e, E3d

→ **Intermediate stage. All the above, plus**
Skills: A1b, A2c, A2d, A2f, A2g, A2j, E1b, E1c, E1e, E1g, E2a, E2b, E2d, E2f, E2g, E3b, E3c, E3e, E4b, E4d

→ **Certification stage. All the above, plus**
Skills: A1c, A1d, A1e, A1f, A2b, E1a, E1d, E2c, E3a, E4a, E4c, E4e

→ **Essential knowledge.** A range of essential knowledge which includes areas listed under a1, **a2**, e1, **e2, e3, e4**

Why is initial assessment necessary?

Your first meeting with a group of students who are embarking on what is, for them, a new programme of learning, represents the convergence of three key components in the learning process: the teacher, the students and the syllabus or specifications of the course which has brought them together. Two of these components you are already familiar with (or at least it's to be hoped you are!). You have a thorough knowledge and secure understanding of what it is the students are required to learn and, through the keeping of a reflective journal, you are coming to know yourself as a teacher fairly well – both in terms of your preferred teaching styles and of how securely your subject knowledge fits the demands of the syllabus. The third component, however, you probably know very little about at this stage. Or rather, you will have information but it will not necessarily be the information you most need to help the students learn. You'll have their names, their ages, their current qualifications. But, nevertheless, these students, in terms of their individual strengths and weaknesses, their individual learning needs, will at this stage represent the unknown component in the equation.

The class known for convenience sake as HNC Computing, or Year 2 Sport and Leisure, or Application of Number Level 2, is unlikely to be an homogeneous group – a collection of people with identical past experiences of learning and identical current learning needs. The 'class' is a group of disparate individuals, each with their own needs and expectations. The following is a list of some of the things you probably won't know about them.

- Why they are doing this current course.

- How their previous experience has made them feel about education and training.

- Their level of confidence.

- How much the previous knowledge they have gained through experience or learning will be of relevance to their current course or programme.

- Whether they have personal circumstances or undeclared learning difficulties that are likely to affect their commitment or concentration in the short or long term.

- How they relate with other members of the group.

- Whether they will seek attention or be reluctant to speak up.

- What activities best suit their individual learning styles.

- Their expectations of the course or programme.

- Their level of motivation.

This is not an exclusive list. You may be able to suggest many more unknown factors we could add to it. What it makes quite clear, however, is that when a new group of students embarks upon a programme of learning it is we, the teachers, who first of all have some essential and very rapid learning to do.

You will sometimes hear teachers talking about the assessment of entry behaviour. This can be confusing for a new or student teacher because it doesn't really refer to behaviour at all but rather to the student's level of knowledge and skills on entering the course or programme of learning. Ascertaining the entry behaviour of a student is important for two reasons. It helps to identify whether he or she will need ongoing additional support in coping with the demands of the programme or initial help to 'bridge' the gap between his or her current skills and knowledge and those required to begin his or her current programme. And, secondly, it can help to identify relevant areas of skills and knowledge the student already possesses, either through prior experience or prior learning – in which case he or she can be advised to apply for accreditation through the process referred to as APEL or APL – Accreditation of Prior Experience and/or Learning. Entry behaviour, though, is only a part of what we need to know about the student, as the list we have just seen makes clear. So how do we go about discovering some of the other information we need about students if we are to be as effective as possible in helping them to learn?

Meeting a new group of students

Let's have look first at what one teacher, Jodie, has to say about the first meeting with a new group of students. The students are newly enrolled on an Access course designed to prepare them for entry to higher education, where they hope to apply for degree courses in the area of social sciences. The module Jodie is to teach contains elements of sociology and law.

Task

As you read the extract below from Jodie's journal, consider the following questions:

- *What assumptions had Jodie made in planning the lesson?*

- *What might Jodie have usefully learnt in the course of the lesson about individual students' needs or prior experiences?*

- *Can you identify any specific points at which Jodie made an unwise or ill-informed decision?*

- *What advice would you give to Jodie about how to plan the next session with this group?*

- *How might Jodie have made this journal entry more useful in terms of professional development and the planning of future practice?*

September 12th

The new Access group. There were nine of them. I wanted to start out the way I mean to carry on – lots of discussion, lots of student involvement. Get things buzzing right from the start. They need to know the course isn't a doddle and that you don't just get into HE by wanting to. And they also need to feel they're getting value for money, and that they're not wasting time and that they go away having learnt something. It was timetabled for room 42 which was a bit of luck because it's a nice room, all set up for PowerPoint and video, and plenty of space to move the furniture about. So I got in there half an hour early at 8.30 and put the tables into rows so they'd know there was going to be some serious learning going on, but well spaced out so they could sit where they felt most comfortable. What I'd decided to do was jump straight in with something that was interesting and that they could probably relate to – and that was the role of the lay magistrate. And I thought we'd have a look at a fictional case and they could get in small groups and decide on the sentence and then we'd see how much agreement there was between the groups. This would get them thinking about issues like subjectivity and arbitrariness and hopefully raise some strong opinions so I could get a whole-group discussion going. I chose an offence they'd all be likely to have an opinion about as well – ABH [actual bodily harm] – a bloke up for hitting his wife.

I'd done a bit on PowerPoint about the role of the lay magistrate and about the bloke's past form and present circumstances which would inform the decision about the sentence. I was still trying to set this up and check it at 8.50 when the first student arrived. She could see I was busy but she came straight over and started bending my ear – telling me her life history and everything else. She was quite a lot older than me and I didn't want to seem rude, but I ended up not being able to take in anything she said and not being able to get the PowerPoint presentation sorted either. The rest of the students started to arrive. When I looked up again there were three women who looked to be in their twenties and seemed to know each other, and they'd gone straight to the back and were laughing. They kept looking over at me and then away again, and I wondered whether p'raps they were laughing at me. It made me feel a bit uncomfortable. The first woman, Tina, was still talking away at me. A bloke came in – white hair, in his fifties maybe – and sat down right at the front; and then a young bloke, who looked a bit lost and asked Tina if it was the right room – obviously thought she was the teacher. And then two other youngish women, separately, who sat down in the middle well away from each other and from the young lad. That was eight. One missing, but it was time to start. I was just going to suggest to Tina that she might like to go and sit down, when she suddenly ups and says to the three at the back: 'Come on, ladies. Don't sit right back there. Come and join the rest of us.' They just stare at her for a bit, and then one of them says: 'Do we have to?' And I realise they think she's the teacher as well.

So I decide to establish a bit of order. I clap my hands and say: 'Right, folks, let's make a start. Tina, would you go and sit down, please.' And then I introduce the lesson. I say a few words about the Access course as a whole, and the standard of work that'll be required. And then I get straight on to the topic of the lesson. Having failed to get the PowerPoint to play nicely I have to just talk at them but I think to myself that's no bad thing because they'll have to get use to this if they're going on to HE. I would've used the whiteboard but because I was planning to use PowerPoint I haven't brought any markers. So I just talk. I keep expecting Tina to interrupt, but she doesn't say anything. In fact she doesn't even make eye contact. So that's a relief. The three at the back just stare at me. They don't seem to be taking any notes. The white-haired bloke, though, he's writing away. Every time I pause for breath I can hear his pencil scrabbling along trying to catch me up. The younger bloke is still going through his bag and pockets for a pen when I'm already half-way through what I've got to say. Needs to learn to be more organised, obviously.

When I get to the specific details of the case we're going to look at, one of the women sitting on her own says: 'They ought to hang him.' I pretend I haven't heard. The white-haired bloke looks round to see who's spoken, and there's a bit of sniggering from the back. Soon after this the last student arrives, 25 minutes late but not particularly apologetic. He sits down on the end of the middle row nearest the door, but for some reason keeps his jacket and gloves on. He's probably somewhere in his thirties.

When I finish giving them the background to the task, I tell them to get into groups of three to decide on the sentence. Nobody makes a move, except the three at the back who get their heads together and start working on it. So I tell the rest of them they've only got 10 minutes so they'd better get on with it. Tina turns her chair around so she can work with the quiet woman on the middle row and the student who's just come in; which leaves the white-haired bloke, the young lad and the woman who said 'Hang him' – and they're all sitting in different parts of the room so I have to sort them out and get them to move their chairs, and finally they're all working – except the latecomer who, of course, has missed most of the background and the briefing. So I think to myself: well, Tina'll fill him in. She'll like doing that. So I go over and ask her and she more or less says: 'I'd have thought that was your job.' The trouble is, she's got this really loud penetrating voice, so everybody heard her say it. Anyway, I sat in with that group so I could bring the late bloke up to speed. Tina for some reason had gone from having too much to say to the other extreme and just wasn't joining in at all. It ended up as a discussion between the quiet woman and the late man – and hardly a discussion, really. He insisted that all of the sentencing options were too severe and that the police shouldn't get involved in 'domestic matters'; and even though she argued quite well that the culprit should at least do some community service, the bloke just laughed. Before I could weigh in, there was a sudden raising of voices in the group with the two blokes in it. It's a horrible feeling when you hear something like that – a feeling like it's all going to go out of control. I got over to them as quickly as I could and found the white-haired man and the Hang-him woman in the middle of a biff, and the young lad bright red and looking as though he was going to die with embarrassment. I couldn't really get to the bottom of it, but it seemed what had happened was that Hang-him had accused the men of wanting to give a lenient sentence because all men sympathised with wife-beaters. Something like that. I tried to joke them out of it, but then she started on this heated argument with me. She was so angry she was almost in tears. So I decided I'd better cut my losses, call time and bring the whole class back together again.

I said to them all: 'So, if you had had the task of lay magistrate, what sentence would you have decided was appropriate? Let's start with you three.' And I pointed to the three women at the back, because they seemed at least to have been getting on with it. They'd decided on probation, with the argument that therefore if he did it again he'd go to prison. So I asked Tina's group whether they agreed. Tina said she had no idea because she hadn't been able to hear a word they said. The late bloke just folded his arms and grinned and shook his head as though in disbelief. When I asked him for his response he said something to the effect that if you started putting everybody who hit their wife in jail there'd be no room for the real criminals. So then Hang-him just went ballistic, shouting at him and pointing, and he just sat there with his arms folded, laughing, and the three women at the back, watching it like a tennis match, mouths open. So I threw up my hands and said: 'Okay, okay. Let's have break. Back here in 15 minutes.' It felt like a nightmare and I was desperate to get out, just for a few minutes and have a think about what to do. But although most of them went off for a break, the white-haired bloke stayed behind to tell me that the young bloke had difficulty taking notes and wanted to tape-record my input but was too embarrassed to ask. So I said to tell him that was fine. And then the white-haired bloke – Tim, it was – started telling me all about how he works for the parole board at the prison, and about the sort of decisions they have to make – quite interesting, but I hadn't really got time to listen. Then the quiet woman, the one who'd been in the group with Tina and the late bloke, came up and asked whether I'd be able to supply her with copies of any overheads or board work because she was partially sighted and even if she sat at the front she couldn't always read easily from the screen or board. So I said that was fine, too. All this left me about five minutes to rescue the lesson. But then I remembered the video on young offenders, which was fairly relevant to what we'd just done. So I raced off and fetched it. It filled the second half of the lesson, thank goodness, although with bright sunshine through the windows and no blinds the picture was a bit indistinct.

Tina and the Hang-him woman didn't come back after the break. I don't know whether to be concerned or relieved. I assume it means they've decided the course isn't for them. You do tend to get a high drop-out rate on these sorts of programmes.

WHAT ASSUMPTIONS HAD JODIE MADE IN PLANNING THE LESSON?

It becomes evident, as we read the journal extract, that Jodie's planning, teaching and classroom management are based on assumptions about the students and the course which, even after the events described, the journal never really explores or questions. These are some of the assumptions you may have identified.

> 'I wanted to start out the way I mean to carry on – lots of discussion, lots of student involvement. Get things buzzing right from the start. They need to know the course isn't a doddle and that you don't just get into HE by wanting to.'

Here Jodie makes several assumptions. One is that the first lesson with a new group should launch straight in to the course content or syllabus, before knowing anything about the experiences, skills and attitudes within that group which might facilitate or impede the process of learning. Another is that a new group – new to each other and new to the teacher – can comfortably cope with 'lots of discussion'. Yet another is that the first session with a group should set the tone and style for the rest, allowing no lead-in time for introductions. When we first meet someone new, in whatever context, we would normally spend some time getting to know a little about him or her in order to pick up clues about how to conduct our interaction. This applies equally to the meeting between a teacher and a new class. It also applies to the students, who are meeting each other for the first time. Jodie seems to be assuming here that the teacher need play no part in ensuring students who will be working together have adequate time initially to get to know one another.

Also implicit within this passage is Jodie's assumption that the students are likely to see access to HE as something easily achieved. This is an assumption about their assumptions! And the chances are it is a quite mistaken one. Adults returning to education are often underconfident rather than overconfident about their abilities. The necessity of impressing upon them that this course will not be 'a doddle' may be less appropriate at this stage than the need to reassure the students and help them to build their confidence.

> 'So I got in there half an hour early at 8.30 and put the tables into rows so that they'd know there was going to be some serious learning going on, but well spaced out so they could sit where they felt most comfortable.'

There's an interesting assumption here that students will equate desks set out formally in rows with the idea of 'serious learning', and that such a classroom layout will signal this to them as they enter the classroom. It is equally possible that rows of desks will remind them of school, or of formal examinations; and Jodie has no idea – and appears uninterested in – whether this will have positive or negative associations for individuals in the group, which might affect levels of motivation.

> '[There] were three women who looked to be in their twenties and seemed to know each other The first woman, Tina, was still talking away at me. A bloke came in – white hair, in his fifties maybe – and sat down right at the front; and then a young bloke, who looked a bit lost And then two other youngish women, separately '

Jodie gives us descriptive information about the students – their approximate age, their manner, where they sit – but there seems to be an underlying assumption this is the only information about them of any relevance. There is not even any effort made to identify each individual against his or her name on the class list or register. They are seen in terms of their gender, age and position in the classroom, as though only these factors differentiate them and that their learning needs can all be assumed to be identical. Jodie's assumption is, for example, that they are all able to take notes as appropriate and that they are all able to see the board or screen clearly. These assumptions can be represented like this:

$$student = student = student = student$$

In the context of student needs and experiences, this equation can never be correct.

> 'I would've used the whiteboard but because I was planning to use PowerPoint I haven't brought any markers. So I just talk.'

Poor Jodie. But there's a moral here. Technology can sometimes let us down. Just as in lesson planning, where it is always important to have a 'Plan B', so with resources. Just in case the OHP doesn't work, or isn't there, and just in case the PowerPoint can't be coaxed to work, always carry a whiteboard pen. And just in case the whiteboard pen dries up, always carry another one! Jodie assumed the technology would work. This is never an entirely safe assumption.

WHAT MIGHT JODIE HAVE USEFULLY LEARNT IN THE COURSE OF THE LESSON ABOUT INDIVIDUAL STUDENTS' NEEDS AND PRIOR EXPERIENCES?

> 'She could see I was busy but she came straight over and started bending my ear – telling me her life history and everything else ... I was just going to suggest to Tina that she might like to go and sit down, when she suddenly ups and says to the three at the back: "Come on, ladies. Don't sit right back there. Come and join the rest of us."'

How are we to interpret Tina's behaviour? Jodie sees her first of all as a bit of a nuisance, a cause of distraction from the job of setting up the PowerPoint presentation. The assumption being made here is that she is pushy and overconfident; and this seems to be reinforced by her appearing to usurp the teacher's role. But look at what happens when Jodie decides (almost literally) to put her in her place:

> 'Right, folks, let's make a start. Tina, would you go and sit down, please.'

From this moment on, Tina avoids making eye contact, contributes nothing to the lesson and does not return after the break. What are we to make of this? Jodie blithely assumes she has found the work too difficult and, in any case, seems relieved not to have her back. But we could put an entirely different interpretation upon Tina's behaviour from the moment she enters the classroom. Perhaps, like many adult learners, she is underconfident rather than overconfident. Jodie doesn't listen with any close attention to the 'life history' Tina is telling; and this is a pity because that 'history' may well relate to her current needs and aspirations as a learner. Perhaps Tina is saying it's been a long time since she was in a classroom; perhaps she is seeking reassurance. And perhaps – just perhaps – her intervention in encouraging the women at the back to move forward was intended to be helpful, to establish solidarity with the teacher rather than to threaten the teacher's position. When Jodie tells her to 'go and sit down please', Tina may interpret this as being treated like a child just when she is trying to negotiate her status as an adult learner. Her own apprehensiveness at returning to learning may well make it impossible for her to see that Jodie's response arises out of insecurity. Jodie is the teacher; and it may be Tina's belief – although we know better – that teachers never feel insecure. From our position as detached observers we are able to see that Tina's behaviour offers valuable clues about her learning needs. This is something that Jodie, even after writing up the journal, has not even begun to consider.

What else have we learnt? We have learnt that the quiet young man lacks note-taking skills and – just as important – we have learnt he is reticent about approaching the teacher to seek help. This means we cannot assume everything is well with him just because he remains quiet. We have also learnt that Tim has experience that may be valuable and is certainly relevant to the course. We have learnt, too, that the younger man has confided in him and that Tim is prepared to adopt an avuncular or protective role towards him. Another useful thing we have learnt is that Tina (and this may possibly apply to others in the class, too) would like the teacher to repeat responses made by other students in order to make sure they are clear and audible to the rest of the class. And we have learnt the quiet young woman is partially sighted and may be unable to see clearly what is on the screen or board.

All these are very useful pieces of information for the teacher. Jodie happens upon them quite by accident when in fact this first lesson should have been designed with a view to discovering these learning needs and all the other information the teacher will need to be most effective in facilitating student learning.

There are other things Jodie might usefully have learnt from this lesson, although the journal extract suggests they have not really been taken into account. One is that the student whom Jodie refers to as the 'latecomer' seems to enjoy provoking controversy. We cannot be sure whether he actually holds the views he expresses, but the simple fact he enjoys expressing them means he is a potential cause of offence to other students. The student whom Jodie refers to as 'Hang-him' also expresses strong views with which she exhibits some emotional involvement. Factors such as these are important for the teacher to bear in mind when planning learning activities and choosing topics for discussion.

Close focus

What evidence is there from the journal extract that Jodie took any of these factors into account as the lesson progressed? What use could Jodie make of this information when planning future lessons for these students?

CAN YOU IDENTIFY ANY SPECIFIC POINTS AT WHICH JODIE MADE AN UNWISE OR ILL-INFORMED DECISION?

We have covered some of these indirectly already. Jodie's rather brusque treatment of Tina could be considered unwise and ill-informed since it seems to result in alienating and driving away a previously well motivated and potentially valuable member of the group, as well as causing a learner unnecessary distress. The formal arrangement of the desks into rows was probably not a good decision, particularly on the first occasion the group met. It did not encourage any sense of group cohesion nor facilitate group discussion. The students were not only not able to make eye contact with one another but some would see no more of their fellow students than the backs of their heads. It was not an arrangement likely to make the students feel sufficiently at ease to talk with confidence about themselves, their experiences, their needs and concerns. A boardroom or horseshoe arrangement of tables would have been more appropriate in this instance.

At various points during the lesson, Jodie makes the decision to discount or ignore certain signals that some of the students may be experiencing difficulties or even distress. There is the decision to ignore the fact that Tina has gone quiet – it's seen as a relief rather than a sign something has been mishandled – and the decision to ignore the young man's search for a pen, which is seen as a sign of disorganisation. If Jodie had paused at this point and offered a pen it might have provided the student with an opportunity to ask whether he can tape-record the session instead. Ideally, of course, the teacher should have ascertained at the outset the students' level of confidence about note-taking and offered help and advice as appropriate, particularly if this is a programme of learning for which such a skill is essential.

There is also the question of Jodie ignoring the woman's comment of 'Hang him':

'When I get to the specific details of the case we're going to look at, one of the women sitting on her own says: "They ought to hang him." I pretend I haven't heard. The white-haired bloke looks round to see who's spoken, and there's a bit of sniggering from the back.'

Of course, we don't know why Jodie decided to ignore this, although we might make an informed guess. Perhaps it's out of a wish not to encourage a potential trouble-maker. Perhaps it seems, as it did with Tina, that the teacher's authority is being challenged. The students, however, do not ignore it. They are probably curious to hear the justification for this rather extreme statement. Some of you may agree with Jodie's decision to let it pass on the grounds that the voicing of extreme views should not be encouraged by providing a platform. In some circumstances this may well be the appropriate decision to make. Here, however, one cannot help feeling that if Jodie had picked up on the comment at this stage and chaired the ensuing discussion, the issue would have been less likely to have exploded into an acrimonious exchange when the teacher was occupied elsewhere. Whatever view we take on the initial decision to ignore the comment, we would probably agree that when anger exploded over in the small group Jodie was unwise to try 'to joke them out of it', since to that group at least it was clearly no joking matter. Jodie's next decision, however, seems staggeringly ill-judged, given what has already emerged about the views and attitudes of at least two of the students. Nevertheless, Jodie attempts to orchestrate a whole-group discussion, apparently blind to the fact this will place 'Hang-him' and the 'latecomer' – two complete strangers meeting for the first time – in a position which encourages the one to goad and the other to grow even more angry and distressed. We might go further than this and decide it was ill-judged in the first place to introduce an emotive issue such as this to a group of strangers about whom even the teacher as yet knows very little.

There are other examples of poor decision-making, too, which you may have identified. How about the division of students into small groups? Would it not have been better to allocate students to the three groups rather than leaving it to the students themselves? This would have provided an opportunity for the three women at the back to get to know some of the other students, and would have avoided the awkwardness some of these strangers might have felt about whether a group would include or exclude them. Then there's the decision to run a video for the second half of the lesson – a decision taken after Jodie has learnt one of the students can't see the screen clearly. An alternative plan would have been to get the students to introduce themselves, to invite Tim to say something about his role or even to have a post-mortem about the group discussion. If we were to ask Jodie what were the relevant intended learning outcomes from showing the video, I wonder what the answer would be? There is certainly a suspicion that the decision to show the video was based on the immediate needs of the teacher rather than those of the students.

WHAT ADVICE WOULD YOU GIVE TO JODIE ABOUT HOW TO PLAN THE NEXT SESSION WITH THIS GROUP?

The essential task Jodie has to undertake in the next lesson with this group is to establish the learning needs of the individual students in order to devise ways in which they can be provided with the support they need. This is what should have been done during the first session with these students so that in subsequent lessons (and possibly tutorials) student progress and the effectiveness of the support strategies can be carefully monitored.

Let's look on the bright side, however, and say this first lesson was not entirely wasted. Jodie did discover (albeit accidentally) some of the needs and prior experiences of these students which will prove useful for planning how best to help them learn. Even though we fear the lesson may have done more harm than good, particularly in terms of student motivation, we now have an opportunity to suggest to Jodie a better way of doing things. Let's go through the sequence of events and pinpoint the changes we would make, bearing in mind all the time that our aim, as set out at the beginning of this section, is to establish the learning needs of the individual students in order to devise ways in which they can be provided with the support they need.

1. If Jodie is going to get there early to set out the furniture, the best layout will be one in which all the students can make eye contact with one another and with the teacher.

2. Setting up the PowerPoint really isn't an essential in this first session. The aim should be to find out as much as possible about the students. The emphasis should not be upon the teacher's 'performance' but upon his or her ability to draw the students out, to listen and to assess. The priority at this stage would be to listen to what a student (like Tina) has to say, rather than to fiddle with equipment.

3. Rather than launching straight into the course, Jodie should plan some 'ice-breaking' activities designed to help the students feel more at ease, to get to know one another a little and to learn one another's names. This sort of activity can be very helpful in allowing the teacher to identify students who may need specific support or who may have experiences and knowledge which can be drawn upon as a resource.

4. This informal activity should be followed by activities that will allow a more formal assessment of student needs and experience – an assessment that can be documented in order to plan strategies for student support. All kinds of classroom activities would suit this purpose – it doesn't demand a test or exam. But the discussion Jodie set up wasn't particularly helpful in this respect. Sometimes the student will have indicated on their enrolment form if they require support in a particular area of their learning. This is the sort of information that it is important for the teacher to possess when planning for students' learning.

5. If the course or programme of learning is likely to require the students possess the skills to make clear and relevant notes during the lessons or as part of their reading and research, it might be useful to build a session on note-taking into this first lesson – as a refresher for those already competent and a chance for others to

learn or improve. This would also be a means for the teacher to identify any student needing particular support in this respect.

6. There may be much more specific advice you would offer to Jodie. For example:

- How would you suggest the teacher handles the latecomer who seems to enjoy provoking an argument?

- How can Tina be reassured and her enthusiasm usefully employed within the group?

- How can the sensibilities of the angry student be accommodated in future lesson planning – and should they be?

- How can Tim's experience be validated and utilised within the group?

- Should Jodie make any reference to the unfortunate first lesson when next the class meets?

- Should it be used as a point for discussion or should it be forgotten as quickly as possible?

Close focus

In what ways was the discussion Jodie had planned unsuitable or unreliable for the purpose of assessing student needs?

You may find it useful practice to draw up a formal lesson plan for the next session with this group, following the advice and guidelines in Chapter 3. If you decide to include subject-specific rather than general introductory material, plan it as though this was an Access class relevant to your own subject area.

HOW MIGHT JODIE HAVE MADE THIS JOURNAL ENTRY MORE USEFUL IN TERMS OF PROFESSIONAL DEVELOPMENT AND THE PLANNING OF FUTURE PRACTICE?

If you have read Chapter 2, you will have seen at once that Jodie's journal entry does not follow the reflective pattern. It describes what has happened in great detail but doesn't reach the second step of asking: what have I learnt from this? Nor the third: what would I do differently next time? There is no attempt in this extract from Jodie's journal to use the experience for the purpose of professional development. It provides us with no evidence Jodie is a reflective practitioner. This is at its clearest when Jodie offers an interpretation of students' behaviour. For example:

> 'Tina and the Hang-him woman didn't come back after the break. I don't know whether to be concerned or relieved. I assume it means they've decided the course isn't for them. You do tend to get a high drop-out rate on these sorts of programmes.'

Torn between feeling concern or relief, Jodie decides to feel relieved. This avoids the necessity for reflection and turns a blind eye to the possibility that such an outcome may be directly attributable to something the teacher has said or not said, done or not done. If Jodie doesn't begin to reflect, it is likely the same mistakes will be repeated.

A final question: did you visualise Jodie as a man or as a woman?

Further reading

Ainley, P. and Bailey, B. (1997) *The Business of Learning: Staff and Student Experiences of Further Education in the 1990s*. London: Cassell.

Harkin, J. and Davis, P. (1996) The impact of GNVQs on the communication styles of teachers, *Research in Post-compulsory Education*, 1 (1), pp. 97–107.

Longhurst, R. (1999) Why aren't they here? Student absenteeism in a further education college, *Journal of Further and Higher Education*, 23 (1), pp. 61–80.

Tennant, M. (1997) *Psychology and Adult Learning*. London: Routledge.

5 MEASURING ACHIEVEMENT: ASSESSING THE OUTCOMES OF LEARNING AND LEARNERS' ACHIEVEMENT

This chapter examines some of the questions most commonly raised by teachers in post-compulsory education and training about the practicalities of assessment. It gives advice on the clear formulation of outcomes and the subsequent selection and implementation of appropriate assessment strategies, and it explains how the preparation, implementation and recording of assessment can be presented as evidence of good practice. In particular, it examines two issues teachers identify as important but which texts on assessment often overlook: how to assess the achievement of individual students involved in a group task and how to feed back to students useful information about their achievement. For a more theoretical exploration of assessment there is a list of further reading at the end of the chapter.

The ideas and advice in this chapter relate mainly to the following areas of skills and knowledge.

- → **Introduction stage**
  Skills: F1a, F1b, F1c, F1d, F1w, F1f, F1g, F1h, F2b, F2c, F2d

- → **Intermediate stage**. All the above, plus
  Skills: F1l, F1j, F1k, F2a, F2f

- → **Certification stage**. All the above, plus
  Skills: F1l

- → **Essential knowledge.** A range of essential knowledge which includes areas listed under f1, f2

Why assess?

This may sound like a silly question. Of course teachers assess. That's an essential part of what we do. But it's worth establishing the answer to this question before we proceed with the rest of the chapter so we can use it as a signpost or a compass to make sure we stay on the right track.

Imagine a lesson which has been so enjoyable the students are still talking about it down in the refectory, and the teacher is walking down the corridor to his or her next class feeling a glow of pride, and even elation, that his or her teaching went so well and the students so obviously had a good time and responded with enthusiasm. Everyone is feeling good about the lesson. But what if – and this is quite possible – in terms of the required learning outcomes, no learning has taken place at all? The students may have learnt other things – that this teacher's classes are enjoyable, for example, or that college can be fun – and these are certainly worthwhile outcomes in themselves. But if the students are not achieving the outcomes required by their course or qualification, the lesson is not achieving its primary purpose.

To put it another way, the teacher's primary objective is to facilitate student learning. A very good way to do this is to ensure the process of learning is enjoyable. But this should not be confused with the erroneous idea that, as long as the students have enjoyed themselves and responded warmly to the teacher, or as long as they have sat quietly and appeared to listen, the lesson has been successful. The lesson has been successful if the students have achieved, or been set on the way to achieving, the learning outcomes – although admittedly this is more likely to happen if the learning experience the teacher has planned for them has been enjoyable and if they have listened to what the teacher had to say.

For a student teacher, or a teacher at the beginning of his or her career, it is usually (and understandably) the case that the focus of his or her anxieties, and therefore his or her planning, is upon the performance of teaching rather than upon the achievement of learning. I use the word 'performance' here advisedly, because the inexperienced or student teacher tends to envisage a lesson as a time to be filled by his or her own activity. They have to be 'teaching' all the time – which can mistakenly be taken to mean doing all the talking, making themselves the constant focus of the class, having to fill any potential silence with words. This, ironically, may mean the students have less opportunity to learn and that the teacher has no time to focus on whether they are doing so. If we remember, however, that the primary objective is about students' learning and that this, after all, is what all the teaching is *for*, we can begin to adjust our focus and to recognise that the careful planning, implementation and recording of assessment are central to what the lesson is about. It's not just about teaching; it's about learning. The teaching is only a means to that end.

If we turn back to the lesson plan we worked on in Chapter 3, we can see clearly that the framework upon which the rest of the lesson hangs is as follows:

Objective/outcome	Activity	Assessment
What the student should be able to explain or do at the end of the lesson	What the student will do during the lesson in order to learn and then demonstrate this	How evidence of student achievement will be gathered and recorded

Lesson plan: framework

The teacher's activity is built around this framework to support and facilitate it. The teacher's activity is never the starting point for planning. Implicit in the framework are the following questions:

1. What should the students be able to do by the end of the lesson?

2. What are they going to have to do to:

- achieve that;
- demonstrate they've achieved it?

3. Can they do it?

If the answer to 3 is 'yes', then (unless you've been teaching them something they already knew) the planned learning has taken place. If the answer, for a substantial number of students, is 'no', that's an indication that, for those students, the planned learning has not taken place, however good the teacher's 'performance' has been, and however much the students have enjoyed the lesson.

Planning assessment

To look in more detail at how we plan assessment, let's go back to Jim, whom we met in Chapter 3. Jim, whose subject is business studies, had planned, taught and evaluated a lesson on planning presentations. This lesson is a useful one for us to focus on because student presentations are a requirement common to many FE curriculum areas and are themselves commonly used as a method of assessment. Presentations are also part of the Key Skills Communication requirement at Level 3, as are group discussions – an area Jim identified as problematic in terms of assessment. What we are going to do, therefore, is to put ourselves in Jim's shoes and plan the assessment component of a lesson for the same group later the same term.

We will take our planned learning outcomes from the Key Skills specifications for Communication (www.qca.org.uk). This is intended to be helpful to you in two ways:

1. implicit in the FENTO Standards is the assumption that teachers' own communication skills will meet at least Key Skills Level 3. This exercise will help you to assess yourself against this standard;
2. this assumption about FE teachers' communication skills arises from the fact that most or all teachers in post-compulsory education and training will, directly or by the example they set to students, be involved in the students' development of communications as a Key Skill.

The Key Skills learning outcomes we shall plan for are these:

- Key Skill C3.1a ('*Contribute to a group discussion about a complex subject*');
- Key Skill C3.1b ('*Make a presentation about a complex subject, using at least one image to illustrate complex points*').

Following his original lesson, Jim reflected in his journal that he had underestimated the difficulty of assessing individual students during a group activity, such as discussion. Now that some time has passed and the students are ready to give their presenta- tions, Jim needs to revisit Key Skill C3.1a to ensure that, this time, he is able to assess each student's ability to contribute to a discussion. He has two double sessions of an hour and a half set aside for the presentations, and 15 students to assess. He plans to have eight presentations during the first double lesson and seven during the second on the following day. He will use the same lesson plan for each of these two sessions.

Task

Decide how an opportunity can be built into the lesson plan to allow the students to contribute to a group discussion about a complex subject (Key Skill C3.1a). You can assume for this purpose that the topic of the presentations is a complex one.

Using Key Skill C3.1a and Key Skill C3.1b, plan the 'Outcomes', 'Student activity' and 'Assessment' columns for the lesson plan. You may like to visit the Key Skills pages of the QCA website to find out exactly what the students are required to do to demonstrate their achievement. You will find the website address at the end of the chapter. Now, focusing on the 'Assessment' column, decide how you will track and record each student's achievement against each of these outcomes.

Outcome	Student activity	Assessment
C3.1b **Make a presentation about a complex subject, using at least one image to illustrate complex points**	*What will the students do?*	*How will you assess them?*
C3.1a **Contribute to a group discussion about a complex subject.**	*What will the students do?*	*How will you assess them?*

Your assessment planning has probably produced one of the following two sequences.

Either
The seven or eight students each make their presentations of about seven minutes which, allowing for setting up, changing over, and so on, will take up about an hour. The remainder of the lesson – about thirty minutes – will be spent in a whole-group discussion around the topic or the qualities of the presentations themselves.

Or
After each of the students makes his or her presentation, three or four minutes is spent in group discussion, either about the qualities of that presentation or about the topic.

Whichever model you decided upon, the 'Assessment' column would show the teacher (and perhaps the students, too) observing the presentations and recording each student's achievement against the Key Skills criteria you found on the QCA website:

- 'speak clearly and adapt your style of presentation to suit your purpose, subject, audience and situation;

- structure what you say so that the sequence of information and ideas may be easily followed;

- use a range of techniques to engage the audience, including effective use of images.'

Similarly, for the group discussion, however it is scheduled, the students will be observed and their achievement monitored and recorded against the following criteria:

- 'make clear and relevant contributions in a way that suits your purpose and situation;

- listen and respond sensitively to others, and develop points and ideas;

- create opportunities for others to contribute when appropriate.'

It is likely the teacher alone will undertake the monitoring and recording of achievement in the discussion as it would be difficult for the students simultaneously to be fully involved and to observe accurately. The assessment framework of your lesson plan, therefore, will look something like the following.

Outcome	Student activity	Assessment method
C3.1b	Make a 7 minute presentation	Teacher observes and records against Key Skills criteria C3.1b
C3.1a	Whole-group discussion about presentation topic	Teacher observes and records against Key Skills criteria C3. 1a

Assessment framework

Close focus

Now we have a clear plan of what we are assessing and how, we need to ensure we have the appropriate means to monitor and record that assessment. Focusing on the 'Assessment method' column, consider what sort of documentation you, the teacher, would need to have with you in the lesson in order to monitor and record the assessment.

This could be done in several ways and the form in which the assessment is documented may depend upon the requirements of, for example, the institution and the awarding body. The teacher may create a separate record for each student, listing the relevant Key Skills criteria, with room against each for a comment about the student's achievement or progress. It would look something like the following:

Key Skills Level 3 Communication Demonstrated during a presentation to the whole group on . . .	Student's name [A. Student]	Assessed by [J. Teacher]
C3.1a Contribute to a group discussion about a complex subject	make clear and relevant contributions in a way that suits your purpose and situation;	
	listen and respond sensitively to others, and develop points and ideas;	
	create opportunities for others to contribute when appropriate	
C3.1b Make a presentation about a complex subject, using at least one image to illustrate complex points	speak clearly and adapt your style of presentation to suit your purpose, subject, audience and situation;	
	structure what you say so that the sequence of information and ideas may be easily followed;	
	use a range of techniques to engage the audience, including effective use of images	
Signed: [A. Student]	**Signed**: [J. Teacher]	**Date:**

Monitoring and recording assessment

The right-hand column may then be used to indicate whether, or to what extent, the student has met each criterion. A comment here is far more useful to you and to the student than a tick or a cross.

An alternative format for monitoring and recording would be to record the progress of everyone in the class on one sheet. In this case the students' names would be listed down the left-hand side and the criteria across the top. This would give a grid on which to record achievement.

	C3.1a.i	C3.1a.ii	C3.1a.iii	C3.1b.i	C3.1b.ii	C3.1b.iii
Student A						
Student B						

Monitoring and recording all the students' assessments

The disadvantage of this format, of course, is that it is little more than a tick-list and therefore cannot be of much use in feeding back helpful developmental advice to the students. Teachers do not always have a choice in the design of the documentation they use for assessment. They always, however, have a choice about how assessment information is fed back to the student, and there is more to say about that important process later in this chapter.

Reliability, validity and sufficiency

These three are the key to accurate assessment. The assessment planning we have just undertaken was relatively straightforward. We had clearly written, externally set criteria against which to judge the students' performance. The criteria were written in the form of outcomes that were observable so that the teacher would have little trouble interpreting them in practice. Nevertheless, even these relatively clear Key Skills criteria may raise some questions in the teacher's mind. For example, in Key Skill C3.1b we are told the student should use 'a range' of techniques to engage the audience. We are told this should include 'effective use of images'. But how many other techniques should we expect the student to use? What constitutes 'a range'? Two? Three? More than three? This matters because, if we decide 'a range' means three and one of our colleagues teaching a parallel class or a teacher in a another college somewhere decides it means 'more than one' and therefore requires the students to demonstrate only two techniques, students whom we judged as having failed to meet the criteria would have been judged successful if they had been assessed by one of these teachers instead. This is what we mean when we speak of assessment lacking reliability. An assessment is reliable if different teachers carrying out the assessment come up with the same result. The clearer the criteria, the more reliable the assessment will be. And, as we have seen, the slightest room for ambiguity in the interpretation of criteria puts the reliability of assessment at risk. In some subjects, such as English literature or the fine arts, criteria for assessment are far harder to formulate without losing in the process some essential component, such as critical sensibility, which is difficult to articulate accurately in terms of observable outcomes. This means that, generally speaking, reliable assessment of an A2 essay on *Othello* is more problematic than reliable assessment of a Key Skill or of an element of a competence-based qualification, such as an NVQ. An essential role of the external verifier or moderator is to check assessment decisions are reliable.

Another important issue for the teacher engaged in assessment is the sufficiency of the assessment evidence. To illustrate what's meant by this, let's look again at those Key Skills we've been working with. One of the criteria for Key Skill C3.1a is that the student should create opportunities for others to contribute when appropriate. But how many times must the student be observed to do this before he or she is considered to have met that particular criterion? If he or she is observed to create such opportunities once or twice, is that sufficient evidence upon which to assume he or she could and would do it again? What constitutes sufficient evidence is often left, in the first place, to the professional judgement of the teacher; but it is also part of the external verifier's or moderator's role to give advice and to make judgements about sufficiency.

It is when we turn to the method of assessment that we encounter the question of validity. A method of assessment is valid if it is capable of assessing accurately what it sets out to assess. If, for example, you decided to assess students' achievement of Key Skill C3.1a by setting them an essay entitled 'Describe how you would contribute to a group discussion about a complex subject', the assessment would not be valid. The assessment evidence you would end up with would tell you something about the students' essay-writing skills and perhaps about their theoretical grasp of how they should conduct themselves in a discussion. But it would still not tell you whether the students were capable of contributing appropriately to a group discussion in practice. The only valid way to assess that is to organise a group discussion and to observe how the students contribute to it.

The more clearly the criteria for assessment are stated, the less difficulty the teacher will be faced with in terms of reliability, sufficiency and validity. In this respect, some course specifications are more helpful than others, and some subject areas present the teacher with more decisions to be made in the process of planning for assessment than others. Where the specifications are set out as they are in the Key Skills, for example, the teacher has a great deal of guidance not only in exactly what to assess (evidence) but also as to what assessment method to use. The method is implicit in the criteria. If the students' presentation skills are to be assessed, the students must make a presentation.

Inclusiveness

Sometimes, however, the learning needs of an individual student mean it is not quite so straightforward as that. In the FENTO Standards, Skill F1b asks we ensure equality of opportunity in the design and application of assessment procedures. In Chapter 3 we read in Jim's journal that he had planned an alternative, but equally relevant, activity for a student called Gaz who might feel unable to join in the class auction. It may well be that Gaz would also find it difficult to carry out a presentation to the whole class or, if asked to do so under the same conditions as the other students, he might be unable accurately to demonstrate his abilities. If this is the case, Jim will need to plan for Gaz an alternative method of assessment that is equally valid and that generates sufficient evidence of achievement.

Let's leave Jim and Gaz for now, though. They probably feel they've been in the limelight for long enough. Instead, we'll look at how another teacher endeavoured to build equality of opportunity into her assessment planning and how far, on reflection, she felt she had succeeded.

Task

Read the following extract from Dorothy's journal and consider the following questions:

- *What concerns does Dorothy express about the reliability, validity and sufficiency of the alternative assessment method?*
- *Are her fears well grounded on any of these issues?*
- *Can you suggest (and give a rationale for) an alternative strategy?*

15th Feb

Time for the Health and Social Care group's second round of presentations. They get very wound up about standing in front of the group, even though they're all fairly outgoing. One or two of them who think they made a bit of a mess of it last time got particularly anxious, and although I didn't want to arrive at a situation where they didn't show up, a couple of them did take time off 'sick' or something – so that now we'll have to keep arranging slots for them to do their presentations later. I'm not sure what would have been the best way to take the pressure off, without letting them think that the presentations don't matter. They're an integral part of the assignment, and the assignment's a part of their continuous assessment. And that's that.

For Claire and Shona, though, to apply the standard rules of presentation wouldn't be fair because of their impaired hearing. For example, they need longer at the end to take questions because these have to go through their signer. Shona experiences some difficulty in making herself understood, and so I needed to find some way around the criterion about speaking clearly. So what I decided to do was to adjust the allocation of time. The other students had five minutes to present and three minutes to take questions. For Shona and Claire I reversed that, so that their presentations lasted only 3 minutes and they had more time to take questions. Shona chose to take and answer questions through her signer, who was able to help me assess how clearly she had communicated the answers. Claire took questions directly, but requested that whoever was asking the question should write it down for her as well as speaking it clearly. They both did excellent presentations and I felt my strategy had worked well. But I still have some worries about it which I'd like a chance to discuss with the external verifier. Was a three-minute presentation enough when the other students were required to do five? Does it matter that I've sort of adapted one of the criteria so that instead of assessing whether S. speaks clearly I've assessed whether she *signs* clearly? Was it OK for me to change the emphasis from presentation to taking questions when what I'm assessing, strictly speaking, is the student's ability to make a presentation? Would it have been better to have secured exemption for Shona and Claire from C3.1b on the grounds of their disability, or would this have been unfair and made them feel excluded? They both wanted to do the presentations and now I regret having tinkered with the timings because I think they'd have been all right without me doing that. I did discuss it with them beforehand, and it was what they both wanted. But I think for the third presentation I'll let them watch the video of this one again to remind them of how well they did, and encourage them to work within the same timings as the other students.

Let's look first of all at the issues of reliability, sufficiency and validity. When Dorothy wonders in her journal whether she should have reduced Claire's and Shona's presentations to three minutes, she is focusing on the question of sufficiency. Is a student's performance during three minutes of presentation sufficient upon which to base assessment decisions about his or her presentation skills? When she ponders on her decision to assess the clarity of Shona's communication through a mode other than speech, she is expressing concerns about both the reliability and the validity of the assessment. She worries the reliability is in question because another assessor in the same situation might have judged it necessary and right to apply the criteria rigidly and literally; and she fears the assessment may be considered invalid because she has used evidence of clear signing in order to make an assessment decision about whether the student can 'speak clearly'. Moreover, the weight of the evidence is about the student's ability to respond to questions rather than make a presentation.

Close focus

1. **What would you say to Dorothy if she asked your opinion about any of this?**

2. **You may find it useful to discuss this case with an internal verifier at the institution where you work or carry out your teaching practice. Would he or she support Dorothy's assessment decisions? It is usually at this level, or at the level of external verifier, that such decisions need to be confirmed.**

3. **Do you think Dorothy should have secured exemption for these two students? What might be the implications of this course of action?**

4. **Early in her journal extract, Dorothy mentions that some of the students are getting into a flap about doing the presentations because their previous experience of doing these was not a very positive one. They don't turn up for the presentations and this avoidance tactic will cause planning problems for the future. In your opinion, was there anything Dorothy could reasonably have been expected to do to prevent this from happening? Could their nervousness be seen as grounds for making some special arrangement for them, such as was made for Shona and Claire?**

Teachers talking about assessment

As we have seen, assessment in practice is never quite as easy as it looks in the text-books. In this section we look at some of the practical issues to do with assessment which newly appointed teachers and student teachers have identified as causing them problems. In the section that follows, we'll focus closely on two of these issues in particular: assessing groupwork and giving feedback.

- How do you assess students on an ongoing basis throughout the lesson - particularly the ones who don't respond very much?

- How do we assess students when they may be starting from different levels of ability?

- How do you translate assessment criteria from the course specifications into plain English the students can understand?

- How do we differentiate between the achievement of individual students when they've been working as a group?

- How can I give feedback to a student in a constructive way when the work he or she has produced is very, very poor?

Assessing groupwork

Earlier in this chapter we saw Jim struggling to assess individual students' involvement in a group discussion, and we looked at some of the documentation he might use to monitor and record their achievement. The question we need to look at now is: how does the teacher go about assessing the achievement of individual students involved in a group project which may involve both research and written work? The answer here, of course, is that you have to be able to identify exactly what each student has contributed to the group effort. This kind of assessment needs careful forward planning if the teacher is to be saved unnecessary work and worry after the event because discovering exactly who did how much of what is very difficult in retrospect. Some strategies that can be put into place before work on the project begins are these:

- when setting out the briefing for the project, the first task required of the students should always be to draw up an action plan for each member of the group, setting out clearly what that student's role and contribution to the project will be;

- the students should be required to indicate clearly on all written work submitted as part of the project which group member was responsible for writing each section, and which group member was responsible, if appropriate, for carrying out the research;

- a final requirement for every student involved in the project should be to evaluate how well the group succeeded in working together and to identify any problems that arose over the allocation or carrying out of tasks. This will not only help the teacher who is acting as assessor but it will also provide the students with the opportunity to demonstrate some of the Key Skills involved in 'Working with others'.

With these strategies in place, the assessment of groupwork becomes much more straightforward.

Giving feedback

It's always a pleasant task to tell students they've done well. It's less pleasant when we have to tell them they've done badly – they've failed an assignment or been unsuccessful in an end-of-module test. And it's not only less pleasant but it can be more difficult, too, because the rule about giving assessment feedback is that it should always be constructive. Sometimes it can seem difficult to give bad news in a constructive way. Let's have a look at this teacher's efforts. He has the unenviable task of telling Scott, aged 14, his assignment is unsatisfactory and will have to be done again.

Teacher: Now then, Scott, how would you say you did on this assignment?
Scott: All right.
Teacher: All right? No, Scott, not all right. You made a right pig's ear of it. You're going to have to do it again. I want it in to me by Friday. And I want it right this time. Is that understood?
Scott: Yeah.
Teacher: Good. Now clear off.

I suppose we could call this feedback of sorts, but it's not particularly helpful to Scott because he's none the wiser about what he has to change in order to do better next time. So let's try again.

Teacher: Now then, Scott. How would you say you did on this assignment?
Scott: All right.
Teacher: Well, I have to tell you, I'm afraid, that there are some problems with it, and I need you to have another go at it, all right?
Scott: Yeah.
Teacher: You've not read the assignment brief properly, look. You've missed out most of task one. And the spelling's atrocious. Do it again and have it in to me by Friday. Right?
Scott: Right.
Teacher: Good. Off you go.

This is a slight improvement, I suppose. At least Scott has some idea now of what he has to put right. But what this dialogue still has in common with the first is that Scott really doesn't get to say very much. He gets to listen, and then he gets dismissed. But what if there are questions he needs to ask – things he needs clarifying? Let's try again.

Teacher: Now then, Scott. How would you say you did on this assignment?
Scott: All right.
Teacher: Well, I have to tell you, I'm afraid, that there are some problems with it, and I need you to have another go at it, all right?
Scott: Yeah.
Teacher: Just have a look again at the brief for task one. Just take a minute now to read it through. OK? Finished? Now think about what you've written here, look. What do you think's wrong with that as a response to task one?
Scott: I've only done the first bit. I haven't put the tables or graphs in.
Teacher: OK. Well spotted. So do you not feel altogether clear about tables and graphs, or was it just ...?
Scott: No, I just forgot to do it.
Teacher: Sure? OK. So I need that done and in to me by Friday. And I need you to look at the spelling as well. Read it through. Spot the mistakes. Run the spellcheck just to be sure. You should try and get into the habit of always doing that. Yeah?
Scott: Yeah.
Teacher: OK. So is there anything you want to ask about this?
Scott: No. Thanks.
Teacher: Well, look, what you need to remember from this is: always read the task carefully, right? Always read the task carefully and always use the spellcheck. Anything else you want to ask about?
Scott: No.
Teacher: OK, Scott. Off you go.

This time the teacher's attempts at giving feedback are much improved. At last we are seeing three essential elements of constructive feedback emerging:

1. the students should be told clearly what the weaknesses are in their work;

2. they should understand what to do to improve it;

3. and they should understand what action to take to improve their performance in future assessments.

Close focus

There is still an element missing – something that should always form a part of constructive feedback. Can you identify what it is?

Look again at that third conversation between the teacher and student. Imagine you were that teacher and reflect for a moment on how you handled this situation. Is there anything you would want to change?

The missing element is this: the student's attention should always be drawn to what he or she has done well, or what he or she has done best. Even if his or her work has not, as a whole, met the required criteria, it will be possible to identify relative strengths. It is important for students' motivation that they should be made aware of their strengths and successes, even if these are only relative. These essential elements in the giving of feedback apply not only to spoken feedback given face to face but also to written feedback given to the student after his or her assignment or performance has been assessed.

How might the teacher, on reflection, improve on that third feedback dialogue? There are two points you may have identified here. One is that Scott remains fairly taciturn. We still don't really know how confident he feels about being able to meet the assessment criteria on his second try. Does he say little because he genuinely doesn't have any questions, or might it be he just wants the conversation over with as quickly as possible? This brings us on to the second point. One approach the teacher might have used would have been to question Scott a little bit more, asking him, for example, how he would go about representing the information in the form of charts or graphs. This would help to reveal whether Scott needed further help on this topic and whether he had omitted that part of the task not through an oversight but because he had felt unable to complete it.

Reflecting on assessment information

Section F2 of the FENTO Standards is concerned with how the teacher uses the information gained from assessing student achievement. It identifies three ways in which this information will be used. It will be:

1. fed back to the students in order to help them with their learning – and we've already looked at some of the issues related to that;

2. passed on to appropriate stakeholders – who may include awarding bodies and/or employers;

3. used by the teacher to evaluate his or her teaching and to identify ways in which it might be improved.

In this section we shall look at this third way of using assessment information.

Imagine, for example, you give a demonstration to your students of a technique or procedure which they then, as individuals or in pairs, must practise for themselves while you observe them and provide guidance and advice. Having given what you believed to be a clear demonstration, you find that student after student is getting it wrong, missing out some essential step or neglecting a required safety procedure. Now imagine a slightly different scenario. Here you give the demonstration and, afterwards, find that only two of your fifteen students have not grasped how to do it. In both cases you have assessed students as not achieving the learning outcomes you had planned. But the use you will want to make of this assessment decision is quite different in each case. In the first, where all students are failing to meet the required objective, it is difficult to avoid the conclusion that something was amiss with the overall planning or the teaching of the lesson, or both. In the second, where the majority of students have achieved the objective, you will need to focus on the needs of the two who didn't. The answer may be as simple as that these two were at the back and couldn't see the demonstration clearly or that they were paying insufficient attention. But the assessment you make of their performance must still be taken into account when planning the next lesson with this group.

Here is how one art and design teacher describes in his journal this process of using assessment information to inform subsequent planning.

April 3

Foundation Photography course, and we were floating the images off polaroid photos and distorting them to achieve effects like mirage or high winds. It's a delicate procedure – needs lots of patience and then a steady hand so the image doesn't disintegrate. I got them all gathered round, made sure they could all see. Got the old patter going so they didn't get too bored while we waited for it to soak. I was working on polaroids of some of their faces, so there was lots of laughing when I tweaked them about a bit to get the distortions. Managed to skim off three quite good ones on to white card. Then it was their turn, working in twos. Not very successful. Only about half the pairs got a result. The others seemed to get too impatient, or were too clumsy coaxing the image off the card. And then, of course, when they failed they got discouraged.

I've got to think of a different way to do this. They could all see what I was doing in the demo. And I took my time, and I talked them through it. I think the problem must've been that I made it look too easy. I didn't stress enough the care that's needed, the steady hand. And I didn't emphasise how patient you have to be, how long you may have to wait before it'll float off in one piece.

When I do it again I'll make sure I'm bearing that in mind. But I'm not sure whether to get this lot to repeat it or whether the ones who didn't succeed will just feel too discouraged about it now. Perhaps I just ought to move on?

Close focus

How would you evaluate this as a piece of reflective journal writing?

Do you agree with the teacher? Should he just move on? What is the thinking behind your answer?

Presenting the evidence

Evidence of your ability to assess learners' achievement can be drawn from documentation produced in the course of your professional practice. There will be your lesson plans, which demonstrate how you express and assess learning outcomes. There will be written feedback you have produced for students. There will be your lesson justifications and your journal. In addition, you will probably have been given written appraisals or assessments from your mentor or tutor or line manager; and you will have access to reports from internal and external verifiers or moderators relevant to the classes you teach. Documentation used for recording and forwarding assessment outcomes may also be used to provide evidence of good practice.

Further reading and useful websites

Reading

Armitage, A. *et al.* (1999) *Teaching and Training in Post-Compulsory Education.* Buckingham: Open University Press (Chap. 6).

Jessup, G. (1991) *Outcomes: NVQs and the Emerging Model of Education and Training.* London: Falmer.

Rowntree, D. (1987) *Assessing Students: How Shall We Know Them?* London: Kogan Page.

Walkin, L. (1990) *Teaching and Learning in Further and Adult Education.* Cheltenham: Stanley Thornes (Chap. 5).

Website

Qualifications and Curriculum Authority – www.qca.org.uk (for Key Skills)

6 METHODS AND STRATEGIES: DEVELOPING AND USING A RANGE OF TEACHING AND LEARNING TECHNIQUES

This chapter suggests a range of teaching and learning methods designed to encourage students to engage actively with their learning and to help you to plan a variety of learning experiences which will maintain the interest of students and meet their differing needs (C1). It addresses the advantages and disadvantages of learner- and teacher-centred methods and suggests some useful strategies for setting up and managing groupwork (C2). It also focuses on learning gained through experience and ways in which the teacher can facilitate this. The ideas and advice in this chapter relate mainly to the following areas of skills and knowledge.

→ **Introduction stage**
  Skills: C1d, C1g, C2b, C2e, C2f, C2g, C3f, C3h

→ **Intermediate stage.** All the above, plus
  Skills: C1b, C1e, C1h, C2c, C2d, C2h, C3b, C3d, C3g, C3i

→ **Certification stage.** All the above, plus
  Skills: C1a, C1c, C1f, C2a, C3a, C3c

→ **Essential knowledge.** A range of essential knowledge which includes areas listed under c1, c2, c3

Strategies, methods and domains

It will be useful if, at the outset of this chapter, we take some time to define the terms we shall be using. First of all, for the sake of clarity, let's draw a distinction between strategy and method. Sometimes, in reading about teaching, you'll find these terms used interchangeably but it is helpful if we assign them an accurate and specific meaning. Let's agree for now that, when you divide students into groups, you are using a strategy: groupwork. The activity you and they will engage in while they are in those groups is the teaching and learning method. For example, you may divide students into small groups (strategy) in order for them to engage in a small-group discussion (method), a simulation (method) or a game (method). Or you may plan to have them working as one large group (strategy) in order to engage in the same methods of learning: discussion, simulation, game. This is an important distinction to make because dividing students into small groups does not in itself constitute a method. It is simply a strategy by which one or another method may be implemented.

Similarly, we must be careful to distinguish between a method and a resource. If we plan for students to watch a video, this is not a method any more than taking material from a textbook is a method. The method will be the briefing that precedes the video (exposition) or the question and answer session or discussion that follows it. The video itself is a resource and, like the strategy of dividing students into small working groups, it is simply a means to enliven, facilitate or inform the learning method you have chosen to use.

In some of the discussion that follows, we shall be looking at how our choice of teaching methods will depend, amongst other things, upon our planned learning outcomes. That is, we shall be looking for the method which will best help the students to learn whatever it is we have planned for them to learn in that lesson. When you read textbooks on education, you will often find that learning is divided into three categories or domains: the cognitive, the psychomotor and the affective. The cognitive domain covers the learning of knowledge, facts and understanding. The psychomotor domain is the learning of practical, physical skills. The affective domain is the area of learning that relates to feelings and attitudes. These are quite useful general categories to use when thinking about our choice of teaching and learning methods. They present, however, a rather simplified typology and should not necessarily be accepted uncritically when reflecting in any depth upon your teaching. For example, where would discovery or aesthetic response be accommodated within those three domains? And how would you frame observable outcomes in the affective domain? These are issues you can explore through the further reading listed at the end of the chapter. For the purposes of this chapter, however, we can use these commonly accepted domains as a rule of thumb when planning our methods.

Students' preferred learning styles

Have a look at this excerpt from Nicola's journal. Nicola has been teaching part time for several years but has recently been appointed to a full-time post. She already has the Intermediate stage of her teaching qualification and is now working towards full certification.

September 29th

Had the first year degree group again today. They're all mature students – all over 21 – and some of them a lot more mature than that! Because they're also my tutor group I'm getting to know them quite well. And I was thinking to myself the other night how well I was getting on with them and feeling really pleased with myself for putting a lot effort into planning the sessions I do with them – making it really interesting, getting them actively involved. And I had the impression they were all really enjoying it. Then today I came up against a bit of a problem with Kev and it's shaken my confidence a bit – not just because it's made me question what I'm doing but also because I just didn't see this coming.

What happened was this. I wanted to get them doing a bit of background reading for themselves so I decided a good way to get this in motion was to get them to prepare for a debate. We'd include questions from the floor so that would mean they'd all have to read around the subject, not just the proposers and seconders, but everybody. This seemed like a really good way to explore

---

some of the ideas we'd been talking about and at the same time motivate them to get reading so they could participate. I thought a debate would help as well to illustrate the difference I was talking about between fact and opinion. Anyway, I was explaining all this to them, explaining what we were going to do, and asking for volunteers to propose and oppose and act as chair. And then Kev, who'd been frowning all this time, starts shaking his head. And I say to him: 'What's up Kev?' And he says something like: 'Have you got a lot of time to fill up or something?' He didn't say it aggressively but I got that feeling you get when you're being challenged – sort of cold and a bit panicky. But I just smiled and said: 'No. But something's bothering you about this, Kev. What's the matter?' And then it all came out.

He said, quite nicely – he was smiling all the time – that he felt they were being a bit patronised. He didn't see why they were expected to do all these activities when what they'd come here for was to learn a body of knowledge. What was the point, he said, in being long-winded about it? Surely it was much simpler and more sensible for me to tell them this information and sum up the arguments than for them to all trail off to the library, all scrabble for the same books, all read the same stuff, come back and debate the issues and end up with a possibly more diluted and less accurate version of the arguments, but having spent four times as long on it.

The awful thing was that, when he said it, it sounded so obvious. And I suddenly felt really silly, as though I'd got it all wrong. While I was spluttering around, trying to answer him, he said that what he expected on a degree course were well delivered lectures – that all these other activities were what you did in primary school and that intelligent people just needed a good lecture. Anything else for him was a waste of time. He was still smiling. He wasn't trying to be nasty, I don't think. But all the others looked so embarrassed, it was really difficult to judge how many of them agreed with him. And I began to wonder whether I'd been completely deluding myself in thinking they liked my teaching and were enjoying the course.

Let's stop there for a moment. Up to this point, Nicola's journal entry is largely descriptive but we'd best not make a judgement about that until we've read the rest of the entry, which we will do in a moment. First, we need to consider what exactly is happening in this situation Nicola describes. Some of the questions we might ask are as follows.

- Is Kev justified in his views?

- How well has Nicola handled the situation so far?

- What should she do about it?

- Should she concede to Kev, scrap the debate and stick to lectures from now on?

- Should she ask the rest of the class what they think?

- Should she politely acknowledge what Kev has said but get on with the lesson as planned?

- Should she justify her approach, explaining to the students why she plans her lessons as she does?

- How would she justify her approach? What arguments could she use?

- Is she right to view Kev's comments as a challenge?

- Should she have ignored Kev's head-shaking and so avoided this challenge blowing up in the first place?

Before going on to read the next part of Nicola's journal, you will find it useful to consider the above questions carefully. You may like to make a few notes in response to each one.

Anyway, in the end what I did was to sit down, with my chair in front of my desk so there wasn't a barrier between me and them (although I'd really have liked one at that moment!), and I said: 'OK, well, let's talk about this.' And I talked to them a bit about learning styles and how some people like to get actively involved with their learning and some just like to have it all set out for them; and how some people like lectures and are great at taking notes and others lose concentration and aren't sure what to take notes about and what not. And I was getting smiles and nods from quite a few of them so I guessed they could relate to what I was saying, and I also guessed they were probably quite relieved I was taking charge of the situation and turning it into an opportunity for us all to learn. Because, on reflection, I think that was what I was doing. And what *I* learnt from it was that I ought to have raised this right at the very beginning of the course – I ought to have seen it as an issue and built it into the induction programme. And that's what I'll do next time. I'll probably use that old Learning Styles Questionnaire that pops up at every staff development session you ever go to. The students may not have come across it before and would probably find it quite interesting. I told this lot about it, anyway, and promised to bring a copy in for them to do next time. Then I asked them whether they wanted to go ahead with the debate, and almost all of them said yes. Thank goodness. But which still left me the problem of Kev. So I asked him whether he'd mind chairing the debate because we'd need someone who was good at taking notes. He seemed quite happy to accept and I think this also helped show him I didn't bear him any ill-will for what he'd said. The real challenge is going to be how to accommodate him and his preferred way of learning in future lessons – because I always plan for lots of student activity. I avoid giving lectures. That's not my style.

Nicola is now reflecting on what happened as well as describing what came next. Her reflection follows the basic model for reflection on practice we encountered in Chapter 2:

- What problem was there? *The problem of Kev and his preferred way of learning.*

- Why did it arise? *I ought to have raised this right at the very beginning of the course – I ought to have seen it as an issue and built it into the induction programme.*

- How can I avoid it happening again? *And that's what I'll do next time. I'll probably use that old Learning Styles Questionnaire.*

Nicola isn't very complimentary about the Learning Styles Questionnaire – perhaps because it does tend to be rather over-used these days – but it can be a useful resource. You'll find the reference for it at the end of this chapter. It isn't the only way she could have found out a little more about the way her students prefer to learn, however (C1a). She could (and arguably should) at the outset of the course have helped them to draw up individual learning plans or contracts which would identify their individual needs, preferred modes of learning and targets for achievement (C1c, C1f). Nevertheless, she's broached the subject now and seems largely to have rescued the situation.

She does, however, raise a very interesting question for us to consider because she's telling us not only about her students' preferred styles of learning but also about her preferred style of teaching. She is more comfortable with using methods that centre on student activity rather than those, like the lecture, where all the focus is on the teacher. We will all, as teachers, feel more comfortable and confident about using some methods rather than others. Some teachers find the idea of giving a lecture rather intimidating – having to speak fluently for an extended length of time with all those pairs of eyes on you. Others thoroughly enjoy delivering a lecture. They enjoy the opportunity to perform, to coax a reaction, such as laughter, from their audience. They may also feel safer when they are giving a lecture. After all, they have total control over the planning, timing and delivery and, in this sense, find it a far less risky business than using a method such as role play or a game where students are given free rein and it is hard to estimate the time needed and impossible to control the outcome. It is likely that you, yourself, will have a repertoire of methods you feel fairly confident about using. If you are at the very beginning of your teaching career, this repertoire will perhaps exist only in your head. If you have been teaching for a little while, full time, part time or on teaching practice, you will be able to make a list of the methods you have used and would use again. A very useful exercise is to list these in the back of your journal and date the list. Each time you add another method to this list, date it. Your aim should be to extend this repertoire as far as possible so that you become confident about using a wide range of methods. The wider the range of methods you use, the more likely it is you will be matching the preferred learning styles of all your students. This flexibility will also allow you to use the method best suited to achieving the outcomes as set out in the syllabus or course specifications and will bring variety and interest to your lessons. Later in the chapter we shall see what can be learnt from the experiences of one teacher who is struggling to do this. In the mean time, let's return to Nicola and her account of how she responded to Kev's challenge.

Close focus

What is your view of the way Nicola handled the situation? Is this how you would have done it? And what about the strategy she uses with Kev?

On the whole, she seems to have dealt with the immediate situation very well. These students are adults, after all and, in discussing the issue openly and honestly with them and introducing some level of compromise and negotiation, she is acknowledging this. It may also be a gentle but effective way of challenging Kev's accusation that the students are being 'patronised'. Should her approach have been different if this was a group of 16-year-olds, do you think?

The strategy with Kev also appears to be a useful solution to the immediate problem. It ensures he will still be actively involved in the lesson she has planned, despite his reservations (C2e); and it also recognises and utilises one of his strengths — note-taking — and allows the group to benefit from it (C1e). However, Nicola still needs to find a way to accommodate Kev's preferred learning style in the longer term.

> But now I'm beginning to wonder whether saying it's not my style is just an excuse. The purpose of teaching has to be that the students learn. The purpose isn't that the teachers do what they feel comfortable with. So maybe I ought to get myself organised into giving a lecture now and again. It might have some real advantages. For one thing, it'll get us through bits of the course material quite quickly. For another it'll give the students a good incentive to improve their note-taking skills – and I'll maybe save enough time, by using a lecture or two, to build in a session on note-taking for those who need it.
>
> Actually, I'm feeling quite enthusiastic about this now. I remember a lecturer we had once or twice at university who used to build a lot of question and answer into her lectures. It was probably to keep us awake – but it worked and it was quite fun. And I also remember she used to use OHTs with the key points on so that we were never in doubt about what we ought to make notes about – we just copied these down. I reckon I could start of with a sort of quiz, like 10 or 15 questions which they have to write down the answers to if they know them, and then I could do the lecture as a way of giving the correct answers to these questions, and elaborating on them. I think that would be quite fun. And if I build some lectures into my lesson plans, Kev (and any of the others who felt the same but didn't say so) may feel better about engaging with the less formal methods, just knowing that isn't all there is.
>
> And I think another thing I'm going to have to start doing is asking the students to evaluate the lessons, perhaps at the end of each week or fortnight. Find out what methods they've responded to best. Find out if they feel they're missing something. In future I'm going to make sure I see this sort of thing coming.

Nicola is right, of course, when she identifies the purpose of teaching as being that students should learn. It sounds obvious but in fact it is possible sometimes temporarily to lose sight of it. Using it as a touchstone, it will always help us to get our bearings when there are decisions to be made. In this case it helps Nicola to realise she may have to abandon comfort and take some risks if she is to achieve this purpose for all her students.

Taken together, the three extracts provide a model of how best use can be made of a reflective journal for the purposes of professional development. The problem is described and reflected upon and then a solution, or series of possible solutions, emerges. In future journal entries Nicola will no doubt reflect upon the success (or otherwise) of her venture into lecturing, and work out where to go from there. The model of a lecture she proposes is an interesting one. We tend to think of such formal methods as demanding that the student 'audience' be passive recipients of learning. But, of course, lectures can be made interactive in all sorts of ways, and this will often add to rather than detract from their impact. Developing and trying out such ideas is one of the more creative aspects of teaching.

You may not have agreed with all that Nicola writes in this third extract. You may question, for example, whether she should trouble herself so much over the idiosyncrasies of one student and revise her methods just to meet his needs. The point here, I think, is that although Kev is the one who spoke up, there may well have been others in the class who were feeling the same – who were finding themselves not able to respond very positively to the methods Nicola was using. But whether that is the case or not, what Kev has helped Nicola to realise is that she was choosing teaching and learning methods according to the criterion of which ones she felt comfortable and confident with, rather than according to her perception of student needs. This is an easy trap to fall into. And so, in effect, when she decides to extend her repertoire of methods to include lectures, Nicola is not simply responding to Kev's wishes but rather is using the incident as a catalyst to move her forward in her professional development.

Learning in groups

Dividing students into groups to learn is a useful strategy, and so let's discuss here some of the reasons why this is so before we go on to look at the sorts of methods groupwork will allow you to introduce.

Task

1. **List what you consider to be the advantages of having students work in small groups.**
2. **List any disadvantages you can think of.**

You may be able to draw upon your own teaching experience for this or, if you are at the very beginning of your teaching career, you may draw instead upon your experiences as a learner. Remember that these personal experiences of learning will always be an important source of ideas and information to you as a teacher.

Some of the advantages and disadvantages of groupwork you may have identified might be as follows.

Advantages

✓ Quiet or reticent students may find it easier to contribute to discussion in a small rather than a large group.

✓ Lazy students find it harder to 'hide' in a smaller group.

✓ Small groups make it easier for students to offer one another peer support.

✓ Students feel less exposed when offering an answer to, or on behalf of, a small group than they would if answering as individuals.

✓ Working in groups helps students to develop skills of co-operation and compromise.

✓ Working in small groups helps to develop students' social skills.

✓ Undertaking a task as part of team helps prepare students for the world of work.

Disadvantages

✗ It can be difficult to assess individual attainment when work is produced by a group (see Chapter 5).

✗ Powerful personalities can dominate a group.

✗ Some students may contribute little or nothing and simply become 'passengers' within the group.

✗ While the teacher is observing or helping one group, other groups may stray from the task.

✗ Groupwork usually involves methods that take up much more time than whole-class, teacher-focused learning.

✗ Students may get bored with always working alongside the same small group of individuals.

✗ Students, if left to their own devices, will tend to form groups with their friends, thus restricting the scope for interaction within the class.

✗ When students have been working in small groups it can be difficult for the teacher to get them to stop what they're doing and regain their attention as a whole group.

There is one further point to be made which is neither an advantage nor a disadvantage and that is that groupwork will suit the preferred learning styles of some students, but not of others, as we saw from Nicola's journal. This means we should avoid making this our only strategy, however firmly we believe in its benefits.

There are so many real advantages to small groupwork – not least that it is an excellent way to get students to take responsibility for, and actively engage with, their learning – that it is worth having a look at our list of disadvantages to see if we can offer some ways to address them.

Some solutions to the difficulties of assessing work generated by a group are addressed in Chapter 5, so let's go straight on to how we might avoid the danger of one student dominating a small group. This is only a problem if it's to the detriment of the other students' learning experience. If this is the case, you might consider appointing an observer to every group and making sure the observer or observers you appoint are those whom you fear might otherwise disrupt the learning. The task of the observer is to feed back to you, and through you to the group, their factual observations of how the group went about their task and who contributed what to the group effort. This serves a dual purpose. First, the dominant student is still actively involved in the lesson but unable to disrupt the groupwork; and, secondly, the students begin to gain an awareness of how their group is functioning and their role within it. Another way to ensure the dominant student does not present an obstacle to the learning of others is to intervene directly in order to manage what is happening in the group (C2c).

Appointing an observer who will feed back information about who's contributed what may also serve to encourage those tempted to be passengers to contribute more to the group. Alternatively, the student who is reluctant to participate, or who finds participation difficult, could be chosen to be the observer in order to ensure he or she had an active role in the learning. Knowing that one of their number will observe and give feedback on the dynamics and the progress of the group often gives students an added incentive to remain on task, even when the teacher's attention is directed elsewhere.

In order to avoid students always working in the same groups, there are a number of strategies you can use to ensure the working groups are not always friendship or clique groups and not simply groups of convenience where students end up working with whomever they happen to be sitting next to. There are several reasons why you might want to manage the formation and composition of groups. You may wish to separate students who, together, are potentially disruptive or lazy. You may wish to ensure that an isolated student is not habitually left out. Or you may wish to place students who are having difficulties in a group with students who can help them. You can, therefore, draw up before the lesson the list of names of students whom you want to be in each group. You can read this out or you could use some other approach (such as writing on assessed work you are handing back each individual's designated group for the next activity). However you choose to do it, the important thing to keep in mind is that this strategy of students learning in groups is something you, as teacher, should actively manage. The success of the learning experience may depend very much on how the groups are constituted and so, if you leave this to chance, you should have a good reason for doing so.

If you simply want to be sure the students are working with a variety of others rather than always getting into the same groups, you might try dividing them into groups by the 'numbering off' method. If you want to divide the class, for example, into four groups, you count around the class, giving each student a number (one, two, three, four; one, two, three, four) until they've each got a number, one to four. Then you tell all the ones to get together, all the twos to get together, and so on. This gives you four fairly random groups and is a useful approach if you need to separate certain individuals to help students improve their learning.

Breaking the ice

For students to work well in groups they need to feel reasonably comfortable with one another. Some of the difficulties Jodie had in Chapter 4 arose, you remember, because collaborative learning was pushed on them before the students even knew one another's names. It is sensible, therefore, to make sure right at the beginning of the course or programme of learning that you incorporate into your lesson plan an activity or activities which will:

- familiarise the students with one another;

- familiarise them with the idea of working in groups;

- establish the model of active learning, where students are active participants rather than passive recipients.

These sorts of introductory activities are sometimes called 'icebreakers'. They are quite straightforward to devise but here are some you might like to try, if you have not done so already.

To help students remember each other's names (and to help you, too), make sure the students are seated in such a way they can all make eye contact with each other, and ask each one to introduce him or herself to the rest by putting an alliterative adjective before his or her name: Confrontational Kev or Happy Helen, for example. It is remarkable how much easier this makes it for everyone to remember a name. A variation on this is to ask students to say their names, followed by four words about themselves. For example: 'I'm Kev. I paint my nails.' Or: 'I'm Helen. I like Star Trek.' Whatever variation on this you use, when all the students have had their turn, go round again, getting them to repeat their line but also to introduce the person on their right by repeating theirs. For example: 'I'm Confrontational Kev and this is Happy Helen.' And then: 'I'm Happy Helen and this is Shopaholic Shona.' And so on. Another variation is to follow this sort of exercise by asking the students to find someone else in the group who reads the same newspaper, takes the same-sized shoe or has the same favourite TV programme as he or she does. This gets them moving around and talking with one another and allows you more easily to introduce collaborative and co-operative learning strategies from the outset of the programme.

Choosing the method

We have already talked about the desirability of being able to draw upon and feel comfortable with a wide repertoire of methods for teaching and learning. We've mentioned, too, some of the criteria you will use for selecting a method. These can be summarised as follows:

- the nature of the topic to be taught and learnt;
- the preferred learning styles of the students;
- the proposed learning outcomes;
- the preferred teaching style of the teacher;
- the requirements for assessment;
- the level of the students' motivation and interest;
- whether or not students have the required skills (e.g. note-taking for lectures or guided research);
- the constraints upon, and availability of, resources.

If you have followed the suggestion made earlier in the chapter, you will already have made a list in your journal of the methods you have tried and feel reasonably familiar with. But what other methods might you try?

Task

Write down as many teaching and learning methods as you can think of, whether you've tried them or not. If you quickly run out of ideas, you may like to have a look in one of the books indicated at the end of this chapter. If you keep this list somewhere safe – on disk, for example – you can turn to it for ideas when planning your lessons.

Now read through the following journal entry, written by a student teacher on a full-time PGCE FE course, and think about what advice you would want to give him.

February 21st

Half-term, thank goodness. I'm supposed to be using this block of teaching practice to demonstrate I can use a range of methods. I've got my tutor saying to me: 'Be adventurous. Make the lessons a bit more exciting.' And then I've got my mentor at college saying: 'There isn't time. You just have to do it my way. That's the way they're used to.'

The trouble is, although he's a nice guy, his way is so monotonous. He just more or less dictates notes to them or makes them copy formulae off the OHP. He's got this theory that dictation is an excellent form of classroom control. He says to them something like: 'You're going to need this for your exam. Take it down carefully. I'm only going to say it once.' And then he says it slow and steady or he puts it up for a minute on the OHP, and they scribble it down, and the slow ones try to peer over to see what the others have written for the bits they've missed – and there isn't a peep out of them. But I don't want to do it like that. For a start, I think the students need to be more actively learning, instead of just writing down everything he says so they can churn it all out again in the exam. What's all that about, anyway? They sigh and look miserable and you can see they're not enjoying it. But he's really resistant to me trying anything else. And because that's all I see him do, I've no idea how another approach might go down with that class. He wants me to do a session after half-term on Probability. And I can think of an excellent way to do that – bring in some dice, get them all shaking a number of throws and recording them, and calculating the probability, and checking each other's scores. No dictation. No talking at them while they scribble away in silence. So I'm going to plan the lesson and write a really clear rationale for it, and see if I can persuade him to change his mind.

The student teacher's idea is interesting but as yet it is only half formed. He's not quite clear yet about his strategy: will the students be engaged in this activity individually, in pairs or in small groups? He'll need to decide this in order to plan his resources – the dice, the shakers, the sheets on which to write their scores, perhaps. Presumably he'll have to brief them before the activity and explain something about probability, then elicit and discuss their results afterwards and reiterate the explanation so it is reinforced for them in the light of their learning. Therefore, although he won't be talking at them while they scribble away in silence, he will be incorporating some exposition into his lesson plan, as well as some use of the question and answer method.

Let's imagine, then, he uses the strategy of dividing the students into groups of three for this exercise of throwing the dice and writing down the score. Bearing in mind the activity will take four to five minutes and that these students have been completely unaccustomed to active learning – in this lesson at least – what do you think would be the best means of getting them into groups? And what would you call the method of teaching and learning which is being used in this throwing and recording of dice?

Since he cannot know how the students will respond to groupwork and since this activity will be relatively brief, it would probably not be worth while asking the students to get up and walk around and reseat themselves when they might more easily work in threes with the two people seated nearest to them. I wonder, however, how the student teacher will move among the groups to observe and manage this learning experience? From what he writes in his journal, we could be forgiven for assuming the seating arrangement for the students is along formal lines – probably a series of rows – which doesn't easily facilitate collaborative work or whole-group discussion of the outcomes. Since he is responsible for managing the learning experience of the students during this class, it might be sensible for the student teacher to rearrange the classroom furniture to a more appropriate configuration, if possible, before the lesson begins.

What should he call his proposed method? We could call it a practical experiment, which it certainly is. But, perhaps more importantly, we should recognise it as an activity that involves learning through experience. Instead of copying down a theorem, a formula or a law from the board or the OHP, the students are testing it in practice; they are learning about probability through their own experience of throwing the dice and watching others throw. There are several methods that encourage or allow students to learn through experience. As well as practical experiments, these include simulation, role play, demonstration and practice, discovery learning, games (particularly communication games) and presentations. You may be able to think of others. What is common to all these methods is the need for the teacher to structure, manage and reinforce the learning experience carefully, and to give the student accurate and constructive feedback.

Close focus

The opportunity for the student teacher to put his plan into action depends upon how successful he is in persuading his mentor that a departure from the usual strategies and methods might be useful at this point. You may find it useful to draft out for him the rationale he plans to write in order to explain why he is planning to teach this lesson in this particular way. You don't need to be a maths or application of number specialist to do this. You simply need to have reflected, as he has, on the real purposes of teaching and learning and on the relationship between motivation and method.

How do I provide the evidence?

Evidence of a thoughtful engagement with methods and strategies is relatively straightforward to provide. Some of the evidence will be in your lesson plans, schemes of work and related learning materials you have produced. Some will come from your mentor or tutor's or appraiser's reports on your practical teaching. There will also be the (written) evaluation you carry out with your classes (C3h) and the written needs and targets you discuss with individual students (C1a, C1b). And then there is always, of course, your journal, which provides evidence of your planning, reflection upon and evaluation of methods and strategies – how you make your choice and how you build up confidence to extend your range.

Further reading

Habeshaw, S., Habeshaw, T. and Gibbs, G. (1984) *53 Interesting Things to Do in Your Seminars and Tutorials.* Bristol: Technical and Educational Services.

Habeshaw, S., Habeshaw, T. and Gibbs, G. (1984) *53 Interesting Things to Do in Your Lectures.* Bristol: Technical and Educational Services.

Honey, P. and Mumford, A. (1986) *Using Your Learning Styles.* Maidenhead: Peter Honey (the Learning Styles Questionnaire).

Reece, I. and Walker, S. (1994) *A Practical Guide to Teaching, Training and Learning.* Sunderland: Business Education Publishers (pp. 108–51).

Walkin, L. (1994) *Teaching and Learning in Further and Adult Education.* Cheltenham: Stanley Thornes (pp. 43–68).

7 COMMUNICATION AND MOTIVATION: MANAGING THE LEARNING PROCESS

This chapter focuses on the importance of communicating clearly with your students and on engaging their interest and motivation. It discusses how the selection and structuring of subject matter should be done with a view to facilitating and reinforcing student learning, and how the careful design of teaching and learning materials can contribute to the successful outcome of a lesson. Since effective communication is essential to the learning process, there is an emphasis upon communications Key Skills in the example material provided. The chapter also looks at the importance to the teacher's professional development of reflecting and acting upon feedback from students and colleagues, and it also suggests some ways in which student feedback may be elicited. As with other chapters, it includes advice upon how your management of the learning process can be evidenced against the FENTO skills appropriate to your stage. The ideas and advice in this chapter relate mainly to the following areas of skills and knowledge.

→ **Introduction stage**
   Skills: D1b, D1c, D2b, D2c, D2f, D2i, D2j, D3a, D3b, D3c, D4b, D5c, D5f, D6k, D7a, D7c

→ **Intermediate stage.** All the above, plus
   Skills: D2d, D2g, D2h, D3d, D3f, D4c, D5e, D5g, D5h, D5j, D6f

→ **Certification stage.** All the above, plus
   Skills: D2e, D3e, D4e, D4f, D4g, D5d, D6h, D6i, D7e, D7f, D7h

→ **Essential knowledge.** A range of essential knowledge that includes areas listed under
   d1, d2, d3, d4, d5, d6, d7

Removing barriers to learning

As a manager of the learning process, it is your responsibility not only to plan, facilitate, assess and evaluate, but also to try to ensure there are as few obstacles as possible in the way of your students' learning. Sometimes referred to as barriers to learning, these obstacles can be as obvious and easy to solve as an over-heated classroom or as difficult to address as a student's lack of self-confidence. We experience a barrier to learning when something else occupies our mind, preventing us from focusing the necessary attention on what is to be learnt. A growling stomach and a preoccupation with how long to go before lunchtime will get in the way of our learning, as will a fear the teacher is going to ask us something we don't know and make a fool of us. Now there's not a great deal you can do about the first (although I do know a teacher who carries biscuits around for just such a student emergency), but it is certainly within your power to manage students' learning in such a way as to avoid the second.

Maslow, as you are probably aware, argued there is a hierarchy of human needs, of which the more basic, such as the need for safety and comfort, must be met before we can give our attention to meeting our higher-order needs, such as developing our potential through learning. The further reading at the end of this chapter will direct you to where you can read more about what Maslow has to say and about how others have applied his argument in the context of education. For now, let us simply keep this idea in mind: that a student needs to feel comfortable – physically, emotionally and socially – if she or he is to achieve his or her full potential for learning.

Task

Read through the following report written by an experienced teacher on her observation of a student teacher's classroom practice:

- *What barriers to learning does she identify?*
- *What could the student teacher do to remove them?*
- *What additions could the student teacher make to his action plan in the light of this feedback?*

OBSERVATION REPORT

Name of student: . . . .

Name of observer: . . . .

Subject: . . . .

Level: . . . .
Number of students: . . . .

Date observed: . . . .

<u>Planning</u>
It would have been useful if you had let me have a copy of your lesson plan for this lesson. I think it would have been useful for the students, too, if they had been made aware of the intended outcomes. You could have written these on the board at the beginning. It always helps if students know the objectives of the lesson - they can put their own weight behind it then, and work with you. The sequencing was clear and logical; but you should consider the real advantages of taking as your starting point something the students are already familiar with. Dropping them straight in the deep end as you did, no matter how carefully subsequent content is sequenced, is likely to cause them some panic. And it was this panic, I think, which lay behind their reluctance to venture any answers to your questions.

Communication

When you couldn't get anyone to volunteer an answer, I'm not sure it was a good idea to start picking on people. Especially when you're not yet familiar with their names. Jabbing your finger towards someone and saying 'You!' can seem a bit threatening, you know. And all the rest are wondering who it's going to be next. And just a tip: when a student is obviously unable or unwilling to answer, you saying 'Come on! Come on!' loudly at them is probably not going to help things. If they don't know the answer, they can't give you it, however much you insist. And if they're unwilling to answer in case they get it wrong, putting them under pressure isn't going to help that either. Well done, though, for noticing afterwards that you'd made Emma cry, although I'm not sure that drawing everyone's attention to it was a good idea. This class is usually quite responsive and communicative. I'm sure they wouldn't take advantage if you adopted a more friendly approach.

Resources

I could have let you have a few more overhead transparencies if you'd asked me. Then you wouldn't have had to cram absolutely everything on to just one. How do you make your writing so tiny? It's almost too tiny for the human eye to see. And I was sitting at the front. Well done, though, for picking up the fact that no one could read it. It might have been a good idea, however, to have apologised to Scott when you realised that the 'strange face' he was pulling was only his effort to focus on the screen. Reading it to them was a sensible solution. But it would have been better to read it from the transparency itself rather than from the wall screen, because having your back to the class for so long meant you didn't see the wasp come in through the window. That was what all the murmuring and lack of attention was about. So it might have been better if you'd asked them what the matter was, rather than keep telling them to 'Settle down.' I'm sorry it was you who got stung, by the way; but I thought you handled that very well.

Observation report

How many of the following barriers to learning did you identify?

✗ The students aren't clear about the objectives of the lesson.

✗ The learning does not start from a 'safe' point with which the students are comfortable and familiar.

✗ Answers are being demanded of the students which they don't yet feel confident or competent enough to give.

✗ The teacher's questioning is making the students nervous, not only because they're not confident of the answers but also because they fear they are about to be picked on and exposed to embarrassment.

✗ The teacher's manner may be seen as aggressive or insensitive.

✗ The students are unable to read the OHP projection.

✗ They are by now too nervous, apparently, to tell the teacher this straight away.

✗ Efforts to co-operate and make the best of it (squinting to see the screen) are met with rebuke.

✗ The teacher turns his back on the class to read from the screen, thus depriving the students of eye contact.

✗ The danger presented by the wasp preoccupies the students to the detriment of their learning.

I like the way the teacher-observer tries to draw some positive points out of all this. And certainly she provides guidance to the student teacher on how some of these barriers could have been avoided or removed. You will probably have added some points of your own. Taken all together, the advice we would want to give him would look something like this:

> If the students had been made aware of the planned learning outcomes and had not been left in the dark, they might have felt less nervous about this encounter with an unfamiliar teacher and an unfamiliar topic. When they failed to respond to your questions, it would have been better to take this as a sign they did not feel sufficiently confident about their knowledge and understanding and to have gone over the topic again more simply or from another angle, or to have invited them to question you. If you don't know a student's name, you should make a point of learning it there and then, and using it. Quickly setting the students a task and then having a quiet word with the tearful student would have been better than drawing the attention of the whole class to her predicament. Never cram too much on to one OHT. It loses its impact and can appear daunting to the students. If the writing on the OHT appeared too small, you could have tried moving the OHP further from the screen and then refocusing. And you could always have carried a whiteboard marker as your Plan B. You should have kept up eye contact with the class. This is an important element in human interaction. If eye contact is absent, for whatever reason, it is difficult to establish the rapport necessary for a good working relationship. And you should have been observing your students anyway so you could effectively monitor how they were responding to your teaching. Signs of puzzlement or boredom are as important to spot as rogue wasps – and more potentially damaging in the long run.

This is a lot more directive than the tutor's evaluation. If the student teacher resolves to take this advice – and it's to be hoped he does – the additions to his action plan would ideally be to:

● set clear objectives and make sure the students are aware of them;

● make a point of learning the students' names, and use them;

● use with care and due consideration the direct questioning of individual students;

- avoid a manner which could be interpreted as aggressive;

- avoid behaviours or interactions which make students unduly anxious;

- make sure OHTs are legible and uncrowded;

- maintain eye contact with the students whenever possible;

- be observant about what's going on in the classroom.

This last point is a key one for any teacher. You have a responsibility to manage the learning experience but you can't manage any situation unless you take accurate notice of what is happening. This inevitably demands you are able to read the situation correctly – to use your powers of observation and your common sense – so you don't assume that students who are straining to see the screen are simply pulling silly faces; or fail to see that all the flapping about isn't caused by an excess of energy but by fear of a wasp. Your ability to observe and interpret what is happening in the classroom or workshop accurately is your most useful asset in identifying potential barriers to learning. And this ability will improve as your experience and confidence increase.

But of course there is more to motivating students than simply removing barriers to learning. Ensuring students feel safe, comfortable and undistracted is an essential first step, but you can't stop there. You will still need to make sure you engage and retain their interest. The next two sections look at some of the ways in which this can be achieved.

Motivating students

You – yes, you – know that learning can be an enjoyable and rewarding experience. You may always have known this or it may be something you discovered relatively late in life, after the age of compulsory schooling, for example. But you would not be here now, pursuing a career in teaching, unless you knew the experience of learning could be a positive one. However, this is not an attitude you can take for granted in your students. For some of them, the experiences associated with learning may have been negative ones: failure, embarrassment, a sense of not belonging, low self-esteem. In the FE sector particularly, we often find students, of whatever age, who have not thrived in mainstream compulsory schooling. Helping them to regain the confidence and motivation to learn is part of what makes teaching in FE such a challenging and rewarding profession.

One of the first steps in helping students to feel confident and motivated is to remember they are all different. We looked at this in some detail in Chapter 4. They may be introduced to us initially as 'Health and Social Care 3' but we must never lose sight of the fact that the group is made up of individuals, each with his or her own aspirations, worries, abilities and experiences. Each one has his or her own story to tell about his or her journey through the education system. Some of these journeys will have been happier or more positive than others. But each student will be carrying the effect of these experiences with him or her, and it will influence the way in which he or she responds to you, to the other students and to the learning process. Now one way to begin to fathom this is to include in your planning those methods and strategies of teaching and learning that will enable you to get to know something about the group as individual students. This cannot be accomplished if, for example, you invariably use the formal lecture, which requires nothing of them but to be passive, silent learners.

Another way to gain some understanding of the individual and disparate needs of students is to undertake a case study of one or two students whose attitude or motivation you would like to understand more clearly. Such case studies are often built in as part of the coursework for programmes leading to a FENTO-endorsed teaching qualification at the Intermediate or Certification stage. Even if that is not so in your case, you will still find this a useful exercise.

Task

The case study should be based upon a prepared interview with a selected student. The interview should be designed to explore the student's learning needs and preferred learning styles, together with associated principles of teaching and learning. In writing up the case study, whether in your journal or more formally for assessment, you should be sure to maintain an ethical approach (for example, preserving the anonymity of the student and others) as you describe and reflect upon the following:

- *the student's attitudes to learning;*
- *what motivates the student and what barriers exist to his or her learning;*
- *the student's previous route through education;*
- *his or her reasons for attending college and choosing his or her particular programme;*
- *his or her perceptions of the college and his or her programme;*
- *what you have learnt from this case study, and how you will use it to inform your future teaching.*

You might first like to read a part of what one student teacher wrote after carrying out such a case study.

I'll call the student Barry, although that's not his real name. I first encountered him last term in the learning support group, where he was getting one-to-one help with his spelling and grammar. I found him a bit grumpy then. And this term he's suddenly appeared in my GCSE English class, and I've been quite worried about how he's going to cope with doing the whole thing in two terms. He's got a lot of coursework to catch up with before he even starts. And he's quite a lot older than the other students, which probably makes it even more difficult for him. But I was worried about how I'd cope with him, as well, because he seems to look cross all the time – as though he might suddenly make trouble. But when I asked him if I could interview him for my case study he seemed really pleased. He was happy for me to tape-record the interview rather than take notes. I told him I'd give him the tape when I'd finished transcribing it but he said he was happy for me to use what he said in any way that was useful to other learners. Here's what he said.

He left school officially in 1987 when he was 16, but he hadn't been attending really since he was 14. He lived in [name of county], then, where they still had the 11-plus. Both his sisters passed it but he didn't, and he says he just gave up then because he felt he was a failure and so there was no point trying. He hated his secondary school because his writing was so poor he was always getting into trouble. In the end he gave up handing any work in at all. He said that, because he always got told off for his work anyway, he might as well be told off for not doing it and save himself the trouble. Because it was his writing and his spelling, it affected his achievement in every subject, so there was never anything really that he could get praised for. After he left school officially, with no qualifications, he went on a training scheme but he hated the college part of it because he ran into the same trouble over his written work. After that, he tried to join the army. They wouldn't have him. He didn't say why. Then there's a ten-year gap where he seems to have been in and out of casual employment, but never very happy with what he was doing. The turning point was last year when he met his partner. She told him that if he wanted to get a permanent job he could settle down and enjoy, he'd have to get himself GCSE English and maths as a minimum. So here he is. He strikes me as quite intelligent. He reads a lot and his spoken English is really good; and obviously he's motivated now to work hard and get some basic qualifications. But he's really not anything like as confident as you'd think he was from looking at him. His confidence is, I think, quite fragile.

In terms of what this tells me as his teacher, I realise I'll need to bolster his confidence and motivation because his previous experiences of learning have left him feeling very negative – about learning and about himself. He'll need a lot of positive reinforcement. And I think it'll be important to make sure he doesn't feel any embarrassment or awkwardness about being so much older than the others in the group. Because his oral English is so much better, still, than his written English, I can build up his confidence in that particular strength, and I'm going to have a word with my mentor to see whether we can take advantage of that strength, somehow, in his coursework. I feel that any minor setback could easily destroy his confidence and motivation and so I'm pleased I found all this out because I'm in a better position to help and support him now.

One of the most important things to notice here is that this student teacher is reflecting on what she has learnt about the student in terms of its implications for her own practice. She is not just exhibiting the curiosity we all have about the lives of others; she is making a professional assessment about this student's needs and about how she can help him to build upon the fragile confidence he has found. This is exactly the purpose of such a case study – that it should inform the teacher's future practice.

Another important point to note is that she has selected a student whose attitudes and motives she is unsure of, rather than a student with whom she feels entirely confident. She is intent on problem-solving here, rather than simply giving herself an easy time. It's interesting to read that she initially saw this student as a potential trouble-maker. Until she had spoken to him, one to one, she would have had no idea that what she interpreted as an irritable expression was probably caused by anxiety. And so we have a clear illustration here of why it is important to sit down with students and help them to plan their learning. I'm not suggesting we carry out a case-study investigation with each student – that would obviously be entirely impractical; but that we recognise the importance of one-to-one contact with our students, even though time constraints may sometimes seem to advise against it. Such contact is essential if you are to be able to help the students to:

- identify their individual strengths and individual learning needs;

- develop their individual plan of learning and assessment;

- recognise what interests and motivates them;

- track their attainment of the Key Skills;

- identify what aspects of study skills they need to develop so they can begin to take some responsibility for their own learning;

- evaluate their experiences of learning and express this constructively so you, as teacher, can respond to their needs as appropriate.

Fostering enjoyment

There are a number of ways you can encourage students to enjoy their learning and look forward to your lessons.

✓ Incorporate a range of appropriate learning and teaching methods so that students don't become bored by the same old activities. Surprise them.

✓ Arrange the classroom or workshop in such a way that you are able to make eye contact with all the students. A horseshoe of tables or a boardroom arrangement is better for this purpose than small clusters of tables where some students may have their backs turned to you. To build up a relationship of trust, you all need to be able to see each other.

✓ Allow humour into your lessons. (Don't rehearse jokes, though – contrived humour can fall embarrassingly flat.)

✓ Use methods that are fun, such as games, debates, simulations.

✓ Give plenty of encouragement and praise. There are ways of encouraging a student who volunteers an answer, even though you're having to tell him or her his or her answer is wrong.

✓ Be enthusiastic. Enthusiasm is infectious. Never say things like: 'We've got to do this. I know it's a bit boring, but . . .' You can hardly expect effort or enthusiasm from students after they've heard something like that.

✓ Show them you value the work they have done by assessing it thoroughly and accurately and giving full and constructive feedback – and by returning it to them promptly.

✓ Make your learning materials interesting. Develop and use a variety of materials that will engage student interest and are appropriate for their level of ability.

✓ Reward success – by giving praise or by organising activities you know the students will enjoy.

✓ Be fair and honest and expect the best of your students, rather than fear the worst.

Fostering enjoyment

Task

Add three suggestions of your own to this list. If your experience of teaching is not yet very extensive, draw upon your experiences as a learner. What have your teachers done in the past to help you to develop an enjoyment of learning?

Take one of these suggestions – your own or one from the list – and incorporate it into your action plan for your next taught lesson.

Materials and resources

We'll take one of the suggestions from the list above and look at it in more detail:

'Make your learning materials interesting. Develop and use a variety of materials that will engage student interest and are appropriate for their level of ability.'

There are three key words here: interesting, variety and appropriate. They are all equally important when talking about the design of learning materials. Let's take the handout printed on a sheet of A4 as our example. This is probably the most common learning resource teachers produce, although by no means the only one possible.

The handout has to be interesting if you want the students to 1) read it; 2) make sense of it; and 3) be able to recall some or all the content. I draw a distinction here between reading it and making sense of it because we've all had the experience of 'reading' something – perhaps when we're tired – and realising that, although our eyes have moved over it and we've perhaps turned several pages, we haven't taken a word of it in. If we want to read and digest something, we have to give it our full attention. The more interesting it is, in terms of layout, style and subject matter, the more likely it will be to seize our attention, even if we are tired. To take a very simple and obvious example, a single-spaced page of dense text is less likely to seize and hold the students' interest than a page of well spaced bullet points, however useful to the students' academic needs you conceive that single-spaced sheet to be. Even if you sit up all night word-processing all the information the students will need to pass their module test and put it all on a closely printed A4 handout, its usefulness is not necessarily something that will persuade the students to read it. Sad but true.

Variety is important because, if you always present the information on your handouts in exactly the same way, the students' interest may wane. As is true in many aspects of life, you are more likely to get their attention if you surprise them. Surprise is a good way to wake a class up and doesn't have to be any more dramatic than an unusually formatted handout. (So put that water-pistol away. Now.) And a handout must be appropriate – to the situation, to the subject matter and to the students' abilities. A well set-out handout that employs a vocabulary beyond the grasp of most of the students is going to serve little purpose except to discourage and demotivate.

Task

Look at these handouts. Identify what changes you would want to make, if any, to the way they are presented.

Key Skills level 3
Apostrophes
Apostrophes are used to denote possession or to indicate where a letter or letters are missing. To denote possession they attach to the end of the word that signifies the possessor, so that if we are writing about the papers belonging to the solicitor we express it as the solicitor's papers. If the papers belong to more than one solicitor, the possessor is signified by the plural and so we express it as the solicitors' papers. If the word signifying the possessor terminates in a letter s, we of course place the apostrophe after the s, but may then added a further s or not as we choose. Thus, Moses' leadership or Moses's leadership. Where the plural of the noun is constructed without a final s – as in children, for example, the apostrophe is employed in the usual way to indicate possession. Possessive pronouns do not take apostrophes. When used as an indicator that a letter or letters are missing, the apostrophe is positioned in the place of those letters, or, more properly where those letters would be if they had not been omitted. So we would write isn't for is not; and o'clock for of the clock; and so on.
Place apostrophes where appropriate in the following phrases:
The sheeps head; the soldiers gun; the judges wig; the womens movement.
Abbreviate the following, using apostrophes:
You are silly; he is not; she would not have; all is well; I did not know.

Handout 1

Nails and screws

Round wire nail – general purpose	Round-head screw – iron to timber
Oval wire nail – short-grain wood	Raised-head screw (brass) – easy removal
Lost head nail – invisible work	Star-head screw- reduces slippage
Cut nail – reduced risk of splitting	Countersunk – general purpose
Cut floor brad – floorboards	Zinc-coated screw – rust-resistant
Clout nail (galvanised) – roofing, fencing	Panel pin – thin wood or ply
Dome-head screw – hides head (e.g. for mirrors)	
Hardboard pin – hardboard	

Handout 2

So, what changes would you want to make? The first handout, I would suggest, makes a relatively simple subject sound unnecessarily complicated by its use of a rather dry and formal vocabulary. It just doesn't communicate very clearly, and this is unfortunate, given it is designed to help students with their Communication Key Skills. The apostrophe is one aspect of English punctuation that follows clear and simple rules, and it's a pity, therefore, the handout presents a potential barrier to learning. Its other drawbacks are that it presents the information in small, densely packed script, and that at least one of the examples it asks students to work on is quite ambiguous. Did you spot it?

The second handout is very simple and straightforward. The text is spaced out and broken up into clear individual points. But it could have been made so much more interesting – and useful – if it had provided an illustration of each screw or nail as well as the name and purpose. The students' grasp of the nail's name and purpose has an extremely limited usefulness if they don't know what it looks like and can't distinguish it by sight from other types. This illustrates one of the important points to bear in mind when preparing handouts and other learning materials: the students can write down names and definitions from the board or the screen if necessary, but drawings, charts and diagrams are not so easy to copy. This is where handouts come into their own. Another way handout 2 could have been designed is as a *gapped handout*. The teacher could have produced a list of the nails' and screws' purposes, together with illustrations, but have left the name of each blank, providing just a dotted line on which the students could fill in the correct name. This would encourage the students to listen carefully to what the teacher is saying, and would also help to make the information stick in their minds, as information tends to do when we have to listen for it and write it down. Of course, this type of gapped handout requires the teacher checks carefully to see all students are taking away accurate information. But it is one of the most constructive ways in which handouts can be used and is certainly worth trying.

Encouraging independent learning

Encouraging students to develop their study skills and take responsibility for their learning is an important aspect of our practice as teachers in FE, and is a recurrent theme in the FENTO Standards. One of the ways we can address this is through the teaching and learning materials we design and use. The gapped handout, just mentioned, is a good example of how we can design materials that encourage our students to listen, to think and to consult for themselves sources of information relevant to their subject. You can try this out for yourself if you read through the 'handout' below. Its topic is the Dearing review of 16–19 education (1996), which has direct, albeit historical, relevance to the professional practice of anyone teaching in FE. Key pieces of information are missing. They can be easily found by referring to the published report (Dearing, 1996) in either its full or summarised versions. By requiring you, the student, to fill in these gaps, the handout pushes you to engage actively with your learning. Alternatively, if the handout accompanied a lecture, it would encourage you to listen carefully for the salient points, and provide a framework for your note-taking by guiding your attention towards the important issues.

The Dearing review of 16-19 qualifications

1. This review was published in 19__
2. It proposed, amongst other things, strategies for more closely integrating A levels and _____s.
3. The intention was to break down barriers between academic and _____ courses.
4. This was part of an effort to promote parity of _____ for both types of curriculum.
5. The government of the day was adamant that the rigour and standards of _____ were to be maintained.
6. A common framework was proposed, comprising four levels. These were: entry level, _____ level, _____ level, and _____ level.
7. The common framework was to be echoed in a marrying of the roles of SCAA and NCVQ to become the _____ .
8. Dearing's proposal for a new AS level was implemented as part of Curriculum 2000, which was announced in the 1999 white paper entitled _____ .

Close focus

If you have never done so before, design a gapped handout for use in your own subject by students whom you will be teaching.

How will you ensure the students have filled in the gaps correctly? In other words, how will you make sure they are going away with accurate information? How might the ways you check for accuracy have other, incidental benefits?

Responding to feedback

Earlier in this chapter we looked at some feedback given to a student teacher by his tutor, and we discussed the ways in which he might want to respond to it. Structured comments like this from a tutor, mentor or appraiser are not the only source of feedback we can draw upon when we want to evaluate the effectiveness and quality of our teaching. We may be fortunate enough to be involved in team-teaching, a strategy which provides an opportunity to discuss and debate with a colleague various practical issues about our classroom style and practice. We may receive feedback on the effectiveness of our programmes from employers, from funding bodies or from inspection reports. However, one of the most important sources of feedback is from the students themselves. Eliciting, reflecting upon and responding to student feedback should be a necessary and integral part of our professional practice. It helps us to evaluate how effectively we are managing the learning process and can provide us with specific information about, for example, what aspects of their learning the students are most enjoying, or how they are responding to the learning materials and other resources we are using.

One of the best ways to obtain clear and structured feedback from students is to design a simple questionnaire and to ask the student to complete it in class so you avoid the problem of chasing up those that haven't been returned. You should formulate your questions clearly and in such a way the responses will be useful for purposes of evaluation. For example, the question 'What did you think of today's lesson?' is likely to prompt answers such as 'Good' or 'All right' or 'Rubbish' – which aren't enormously helpful. On the other hand, questions such as 'Indicate which one of the following activities you found most useful in today's lesson: small group discussion; role play; lecture; and 'Explain in one sentence why you found that most useful' are more likely to provide the sort of information that will be helpful to you in future planning.

Task

Look carefully at these two examples of student evaluation forms and consider the extent to which they would be effective in eliciting feedback that is useful to the teacher.

Student Evaluation

Please answer each of the questions with a "Yes" or a "No"

1. The introduction to the lesson gained and held my attention.

2. The introduction told me clearly what the lesson was going to be about.

3. The introduction told me what would be expected of me in the lesson.

4. I felt comfortable about taking an active part in the lesson.

5. The teacher asked questions in a way that made me feel comfortable about answering.

6. I found the lesson interesting.

7. The lesson provided sufficient information for me to begin my assignment.

Thank you for completing this questionnaire.

Student evaluation form (a)

Student Evaluation Sheet

Please take time to answer the following questions as honestly as possible. You do not have to give your name.

1. Did you enjoy the group work after the lecture?

    Yes ☐   No ☐

If yes, why? If no, why not?

_____

_____

2. Did you enjoy the discussion which followed the group work?

    Yes ☐   No ☐

If yes, why? If no, why not?

_____

_____

3. Do you feel you learnt anything useful from the group work and the discussion?

    Yes ☐   No ☐

If yes, what do you think you learnt? If not, why not?

_____

_____

Thank you.

Student evaluation form (b)

Both these questionnaires, though different in approach and layout, are going to provide the teacher with useful information. The first (a) is very simple. The advantage of this is that it shouldn't present a barrier to students. The unelaborated, 'yes' or 'no' answers will provide only limited information, however. For example, the teacher won't know *why* the student might have felt uncomfortable or found the lesson uninteresting. This presents a problem when using the evaluation to inform future planning.

The second (b) overcomes this difficulty by providing a space for the students to elaborate on their answers. It is, sensibly, a very limited space, so the student doesn't feel daunted by the prospect of making a response. This questionnaire also promises anonymity so the students will feel they can answer the questions honestly. It seems to be designed to give the teacher a better idea of the students' preferred styles of learning, whereas the first questionnaire would be more likely to help evaluate the students' responses to the teacher's style of teaching.

Presenting the evidence

Evidence of your ability to manage the learning process will be naturally generated by your adherence to good practice. It will consist of written feedback from tutors, mentors and others; of student evaluations; and of the materials and resources you produce to facilitate learning. But above all, there must be evidence of your ability to reflect upon and respond to feedback from all sources. This will be found in your planning, your journal and your ongoing action plan.

Further reading and useful websites

Reading

Armitage, A. et al. (1999) *Teaching and Training in Post-Compulsory Education.* Buckingham: Open University Press (Chap. 4).

Curzon, L. B. (1997) *Teaching in FE: An Outline of Principles and Practice.* London: Cassell.

Dearing, R. (1996) *Review of Qualifications for 16–19-Year-Olds.* London: SCAA.

Mager, R. (1991) *Developing Attitude toward Learning.* London: Kogan Page.

Maslow, A. (1987) *Motivation and Personality.* New York: Harper & Row.

Unwin, L. and Wellington, J. (2000) *Young People's Perspectives on Education, Training and Employment.* London: Kogan Page.

Websites

Department for Education and Employment – www.dfee.gov.uk
Qualifications and Curriculum Authority – www.qca.org.uk

8 PROFESSIONALISM AND SCHOLARSHIP: MEETING PROFESSIONAL REQUIREMENTS

This chapter draws upon those that have gone before in order to explore what we mean by professionalism in the context of FE. It examines how professionalism is demonstrated in our day-to-day practice, and it makes close links with Chapter 2 in arguing that professionalism is enhanced by reflective practice. In addressing the role scholarship plays in the continuing development of the professional educator, it encourages the reader to identify and reflect upon some key philosophical issues as a means of examining his or her own professional values. The discussion in this chapter is relevant, therefore, to all areas of the FENTO Standards but it draws directly on the following areas of skills and knowledge.

- → **Introduction stage**
  Skills: **H1b, H1c, H1d, H1f, H1h, H1k, H2b, H2d, H2e, H2h, H2i**

- → **Intermediate stage. All the above, plus**
  Skills: **H1a, H1e, H1j, H2a, H2c, H2f, H2g**

- → **Certification stage. All the above**

- → **Essential knowledge.** A range of essential knowledge which includes areas listed under **h1, h2**

What do we mean by professionalism?

The FENTO Standards draw our attention to two aspects of professionalism: one is about applying a set of values (H1); the other is about conforming to a code of practice (H2). Central to both is the ability to recognise, and take responsibility for supporting, the rights and needs of learners. One of things this chapter sets out to do is to encourage you to identify and reflect upon your own professional values. We began this process in Chapter 2 when you were asked to think about your 'best teacher'. In a sense, your best teacher will embody a set of values about teaching and learning you yourself believe to be both important and valid. You may never have articulated those values, even to yourself, but they are implicit in the very fact you see this teacher as 'The Best'. Perhaps he or she showed genuine concern for his or her students. Or perhaps he or she kept excellent order in the classroom. Whatever his or her virtues, in choosing him or her you are recognising that these represent values you approve of and share. But of course, a set of professional values is more complicated than this. Another way to think about it is to ask yourself:

- What is my philosophy of teaching and learning?

- What do I believe is the purpose of education?

- What is the teacher's role in the process of learning?

- What is my understanding of the power relationships involved?

- Where does my responsibility begin and end?

These are some of the questions we shall be wrestling with as this chapter proceeds.

Conforming to a code of professional practice is, by comparison, rather more straightforward. For while our values represent something internal to us – a part of our own moral and ethical guidance system – the code of practice to which we conform is external, embedded in the framework of the college's rules, regulations and duties of care to learners and to others. Such a code will require us, for example, to conduct ourselves in an appropriate and professional manner while carrying out our duties. In this instance our internalised set of values (if we have 10 grams of common sense) will be telling us exactly the same. If we have chosen the right profession or the right institution, our own value base will generally support the agreed codes of professional practice within which we have to operate.

Working within a professional value base

In previous chapters we have encountered a range of teachers whom we have come to know through the pages of their reflective journals. As you were reading those journal extracts, it is likely you were drawing inferences about the teachers' individual philosophies or value systems from the way they prioritised their concerns or the manner in which they wrote about their students, or the degree to which they were able and willing to reflect on their experiences.

Jim, who writes in Chapter 3 about his experience of holding an 'auction', reveals something about his professional values in what he writes. He believes, for example, that students can be better motivated if he makes the learning experience novel and fun. He believes that such risk-taking is worth while in the interests of student learning. And the contingency plan he makes for Gaz shows us he accepts a responsibility for ensuring all students are actively engaged in the learning experience, according to their needs or abilities. Dorothy, too, in Chapter 5, demonstrates that a concern with inclusiveness is one of her central values, as she reflects on how best to accommodate the assessment needs of Shona and Claire when they make their presentations. She also shows us she believes students' performance and confidence can be enhanced by encouraging them to focus on their achievements and successes rather than their difficulties or failures – as when she plans to show Shona and Claire the video of their successful presentations. And from the evidence of their journal extracts we can see that both Jim and Dorothy place a high value on reflective practice.

Close focus

Looking back at your last journal entry (or at the last lesson you taught or attended), you should begin to identify (if you have not done so already) some of the beliefs or values that inform your own teaching.

The professional values you hold will not relate exclusively to your teaching. They will inform the way in which you interact with colleagues and other professionals; your engagement with your specialist subject; and your relationship to the institution in which you teach (and learn). We shall consider this wider context in the later part of this chapter. For the time being, however, we will focus on identifying the values we bring to our teaching. We don't have to read philosophy books to do this – although it's interesting to do so and reading what philosophers have to say is an extremely useful way of reflecting on our own values and beliefs. In fact, as the philosopher Richard Rorty (1989) points out, we can look at literature of all kinds, including fiction, in order to trigger our thought processes into examining what we do or do not believe – in our case, about teaching, learning and student motivation.

Task

Read the following extracts carefully and consider these questions. They require quite lengthy answers and so you may find it useful to make notes.

1. **What theories or philosophies about education are implicit in each extract? (You don't need to come up with 'official' names for them -- just describe them.) In other words, what is being suggested here about the nature and purpose of education? What underlying values are suggested?**

2. **What is your personal view about these theories and values?**

3. **What arguments would you construct if you wished to disagree or agree with each or any of them?**

4. **Just out of interest, can you identify the sources of the extracts? (There are lots of clues in the texts themselves.)**

'Now, what I want is, Facts. Teach these boys and girls nothing but Facts. Facts alone are wanted in life. Plant nothing else and root out everything else. You can only form the minds of reasoning animals upon Facts; nothing else will ever be of any service to them. This is the principle on which I bring up my own children. Stick to facts, sir!'

The scene was a plain, bare, monotonous vault of a schoolroom, and the speaker's square forefinger emphasized his observations by underscoring every sentence with a line on the schoolmaster's sleeve.

'In this life, we want nothing but Facts, sir; nothing but Facts!'

The speaker, and the schoolmaster, and the third grown person present, all backed a little, and swept with their eyes the inclined plane of little vessels then and there arranged in order, ready to have imperial gallons of facts poured into them until they were full to the brim

'Girl number twenty,' said Mr Gradgrind, squarely pointing with his square forefinger, 'I don't know that girl. Who is that girl?'

'Sissy Jupe, sir,' explained number twenty, blushing, standing up, and curtseying.

'Sissy is not a name,' said Mr Gradgrind. 'Don't call yourself Sissy. Call yourself Cecilia.'

'It's father as calls me Sissy, sir,' returned the young girl in a trembling voice, and with another curtsey.

'Then he has no business to do it,' said Mr Gradgrind. 'Tell him he mustn't. Cecilia Jupe. Let me see. What is your father?'

'He belongs to the horse-riding, if you please, sir.'

Mr Gradgrind frowned, and waved off the objectionable calling with his hand.

'We don't want to know anything about that here. You mustn't tell us about that here. Your father breaks horses, don't he?'

'If you please, sir, when they can get any to break, they do break horses in the ring, sir.'

'You mustn't tell us about the ring here. Very well, then. Describe your father as a horse-breaker. He doctors sick horses, I dare say?'

'Oh yes, sir.'

'Very well, then. He is a veterinary surgeon, a farrier and horse-breaker. Give me your definition of a horse.'

(Sissy Jupe thrown into the greatest alarm by this demand.)

'Girl number twenty unable to define a horse!' said Mr Gradgrind, for the general behoof of all the little pitchers. 'Girl number twenty possessed of no facts, in reference to one of the commonest of animals! Some boy's definition of a horse. Bitzer, yours.'

The square finger, moving here and there, lighted suddenly on Bitzer, perhaps because he chanced to sit in the same ray of sunlight which, darting in at one of the bare windows of the intensely white-washed room, irradiated Sissy. For, the boys and girls sat on the face of the inclined plane in two compact bodies, divided up the centre by a narrow interval

'Bitzer,' said Thomas Gradgrind. 'Your definition of a horse.'

'Quadruped. Gramniverous. Forty teeth, namely twenty-four grinders, four eye-teeth, and twelve incisive. Sheds coat in the spring; in marshy countries, sheds hoofs, too. Hoofs hard, but requiring to be shod with iron. Age known by marks in mouth.' Thus (and much more) Bitzer.

'Now girl number twenty,' said Mr Gradgrind. 'You know what a horse is.'

There are plenty of clues in this passage which tell us the scene described happened a long time ago. But we would be foolish to dismiss it simply on those grounds as irrelevant. There are theories of education and of learning implicit in this passage which are still alive and well today. You may have recognised some of them.

Let's look first at Mr Gradgrind's contention that education is about instilling facts. Whether you agree or disagree, this is certainly an idea worth unpicking. Defining education as the transmission of facts has many practical advantages. It is very easy to measure student achievement because the outcomes are completely straightforward – the student either knows the facts or doesn't. Similarly, it is a simple matter to judge whether the teacher has succeeded – whether his or her teaching has been effective – by whether the students know the facts or not. This idea of the teacher as a transmitter of facts, or that extension of facts we call 'knowledge', is still current. Consider the metaphor, widely used today but seldom heard thirty years ago, of the teacher as someone who *delivers*: delivers a lesson, delivers the curriculum, delivers the facts. Most teachers accept this metaphor without a second thought. But what if it is telling us something very important about how the role of the teacher is currently construed? Lakoff and Johnson (1980) argue that the metaphors we use reflect the way we see things. So, as a profession, do we simply deliver the curriculum or do we help shape and develop it? Do we just deliver lessons or do we carefully plan, implement and reflect upon how we facilitate student learning?

Did you notice that Gradgrind's students are described, on two occasions, as 'vessels' or 'pitchers'? This idea of the learner as an empty vessel waiting to be filled up by knowledge or 'facts' is certainly still with us. The South American educator, Paulo Freire (1972), described this as the banking model of education in which students come to the teacher and 'withdraw' a body of knowledge they can then take away with them and consider themselves 'educated'. Freire argues this model is fundamentally flawed. A close reading of the passage about Mr Gradgrind's teaching may lead us to agree.

For example, if we were to accept that learning is simply about the transmission of knowledge – about filling up empty pitchers – we would want to ask: who defines knowledge? Who decides what is going to be included in that body of knowledge and what will be left out? According to what criteria will such a decision be made? And to what ends? It's quite clear from the passage we've just read that only Gradgrind's definition of what constitutes knowledge is allowed in his classroom. Sissy's experiential knowledge of horses – which may include the intelligence with which they respond to humans or how it feels and sounds to watch them race at a gallop – is inadmissible. It is not counted as knowledge because knowledge is only what Gradgrind defines it to be. And this is extended even to reconstructing the student's reality. Sissy's father is a performer: he rides horses in the ring. But this is unacceptable to Gradgrind, who insists the man must be described as a vet, farrier and horse-breaker. Thus redefined, the man's real occupation – too frivolous for Gradgrind's taste – becomes invisible. There is a very important issue here, and it is about power. Who defines what is legitimate knowledge? You? Mr Gradgrind? The awarding body? The Department for Education and Employment? Who decides what you teach and what you leave out? On what grounds is that decision made? Is legitimate knowledge that which will qualify the student to serve the needs of the economy? Is it also that which allows the student to develop his or her creative or artistic potential for purely personal ends? Who decides? And are these two purposes equally important? Would legitimate knowledge include the skills to question the purposes of education itself? These questions are slippery; which is to say they are hard to get a grip on and difficult to answer definitively, without feeling some degree of ambivalence. But they are questions which, as professionals in education, we need to engage with, discuss and reflect upon.

As well as a theory about what constitutes education, we also learn something from the extract about Gradgrind's theories of classroom practice. When he picks on Bitzer, he provides us with a classic example of what I have heard some trainers describe as the Pose, Pause and Pounce:

• he poses the question: '*Some boy's definition of a horse*';

- he pauses – *the square finger moving here and there*;

- and then he pounces: *'Bitzer, yours.'*

The idea here is to seize every student's attention. All are struggling to come up with an answer in case they are the ones pounced on. All eyes will be on the teacher. Everyone will be a little on edge, wondering, 'Will it be me?' and possibly hoping very much it won't be. The 'trick', so I'm told, is to pick on someone who's avoiding your eye, because if he or she is looking straight at you, that probably means he or she knows the answer. So you pick some poor soul who looks as though he or she doesn't know it and then, so the reasoning goes, he or she will make pretty sure they know the answer the next time in order to avoid humiliation. Now, although it may have its occasional uses, I'm not very keen on this idea, and not just because it's one Gradgrind uses. It seems to me that it's based on the theory that students can be motivated by fear – of embarrassment, failure or humiliation – and, of course, they can. But there are much better ways of motivating them, as we've seen from some of the journals we've dipped into; and a personal theory of teaching which is not underpinned by values of concern for, and care towards, the learner, will limit rather than enhance the teacher's professional practice. However, such values are clearly not a part of Gradgrind's philosophy, as evidenced by the fact his student is a number to him rather than a name. He only engages with Sissy's name in order to correct it.

So how well do you know your students' names? How quickly do you learn them? Do you make an active effort to learn names when you first encounter a class? (We looked at some interesting ways to do this in Chapter 6.) Addressing students by name, and getting it right, may sound too obvious a thing to mention. But if you've ever encountered a teacher who doesn't, you'll have first-hand experience of how that makes a student feel.

You may well have identified other ideas and theories from this passage you'll want to discuss or reflect upon and, if you are working alone, you can use your journal to do this. As we leave Mr Gradgrind, however, I will, out of deference to him, point out one interesting *fact*. The inclined plane of boys and girls, which is twice mentioned, refers to the custom, common in the nineteenth century, of seating pupils in a 'gallery' of raised tiers rather like a lecture theatre so the teacher, down at the front, could see all of them clearly at all times. You may like to reflect on what that tells us about the educational theories and values of the time.

> ' "All of you in this city are brothers," is what we shall tell them. "But the gods as they were making you, put gold in those of you with the capacity to rule; and so those are deserving of most respect. They put silver in those who are auxiliaries, and iron and copper in the farmers and craftsmen. In most cases your children are of the same nature as yourselves, but because you are all closely related sometimes a silver offspring will come from gold, or a gold one from silver, and so on. Therefore the primary and most important command of the gods to the rulers is that they should be good guardians and watch carefully over their offspring, seeing which of those metals is mixed in their souls. And if their own offspring has a mixture of

copper or iron, they must make no exception, but must do what is proper to its nature, and set it among the artisans or the farmers. If, on the other hand, in these lower classes children are born with a mixture of gold and silver, the rulers must do the right thing and appoint the first to be guardians and the second to be auxiliaries. For it is prophesied that the city shall perish if it is defended only by iron or copper.'' Is there any trickery we can use to persuade them to believe this story?'

'No,' he said, 'it cannot hope to succeed with your original citizens. But possibly their sons and grandsons, and future generations, might believe it.'

'Very well,' I said. 'That would still be advantageous if it made them loyal to the city and to each other.'

This passage, sometimes known as the *Myth of the Mixed Metals*, is a famous one. Considered in the context of a philosophy for education, it can appear to us today quite chilling. The citizens are to be told they are born with particular qualities that determine their position and role in the social hierarchy. They are to be told this is the way it was meant to be. This fiction is a conscious lie, designed to maintain social stability. Even so, it isn't too difficult to relate this to some of the ideas about education which were prevalent even in the last century. The tripartite system of secondary education introduced by the Education Act 1944 (sometimes called the Butler Act) was based on the premise that, by the age of 11 years, it would be possible to judge whether a child was best fitted for a grammar, a secondary modern or a technical education. Despite rhetoric at the time about parity of esteem, these three routes were never in reality accorded equal status. The subsequent debate about the relative merits of selective and comprehensive education has never gone away, and seems currently to be gaining a new impetus. Curriculum 2000 (C2K) has brought the Advanced Level GCE and GNVQ into a closer relationship, but many issues about status remained largely unresolved.

This extract also describes the possibility of 'children of silver' being born from 'parents of gold', and vice versa. It is a discussion we still have today when we wonder about how much of our behaviour and ability is inherent when we are born, and how much is learnt. This is often referred to as the Nature-Nurture debate and, despite the continuing growth of research into genetics, it, too, has not been definitively resolved.

Within these contexts, then, some of the questions the passage may have raised for you are these:

- Are students' innate abilities fixed?

- Is it useful to group students according to their level of ability?

- How can their level of ability be reliably judged?

- Who sets the criteria?

- What is the conceptual difference between grouping students according to 'ability' and grouping them according to 'need'? (In other words, how might it change our thinking – and our practice – if we used the word 'need' instead of 'ability'?)

- What is the nature of the link between academic assessment and maintaining the social structure?

- To what extent is the purpose of education to serve society and strengthen the economy?

- Does education have any other purpose?

- Is there any difference, perceived or apparent, within your institution between the status of A-level and AVCE students, or NVQ candidates and those enrolled on C2K courses?

- How do we, as teachers, judge a student's potential and provide appropriate guidance?

- To what extent does your knowledge of students' backgrounds and home circumstances affect the initial judgements you make about their needs, abilities or potential?

These are difficult and sometimes controversial questions. All of them have been explored extensively in the literature on education, and some guidance for reading about them in more depth is provided at the end of this chapter.

Although Mr Bonnycastle was severe, he was very judicious. Mischief of all kinds was visited but by slender punishment, such as being kept in at play hours, &c and he seldom interfered with the boys for fighting, although he checked decided oppression. The great *sine qua non** for him was attention to their studies. He soon discovered the capabilities of his pupils, and he forced them accordingly; but the idle boy, the bird who 'could sing and wouldn't sing', received no mercy. The consequence was, that he turned out the cleverest boys, and his conduct was so uniform and unvarying in its tenor, that if he was feared when they were under his control, he was invariably liked by those whom he had instructed, and they continued his friends in after life.

Mr Bonnycastle at once perceived that it was no use coaxing our hero, and that fear was the only attribute by which he could be controlled. So, as soon as Dr Middleton had quitted the room, he addressed him in a commanding tone, 'Now, boy, what is your name?'

'Johnny.'

'And what is your other name, sir?'

Jack, who appeared to repent his condescension, did not at first answer; but he looked again in Mr Bonnycastle's face, and then round the room; there was no one to help him, and he could not help himself, so he replied, 'Easy.'

'Do you know why you are sent to school?'

'Scolding father.'

'No; you are sent to learn to read and write.'

'But I won't read and write,' replied Jack, sulkily.

'Yes, you will; and you are going to read your letters now directly.'

Jack made no answer. Mr Bonnycastle opened a sort of bookcase, and displayed to John's astonished view a series of canes, ranged up and down like billiard cues, and continued, 'Do you know what those are for? They are to teach little boys to read and write, and now I am going to teach you. You'll soon learn. Look now here,' continued Mr Bonnycastle, opening a book with large type, and taking a capital at the head of a chapter, about half an inch long. 'Do you see that letter?'

'Yes,' replied Johnny, turning his eyes away, and picking his fingers.

'Well, that is the letter B. Do you see it? Look at it so that you may know it again. That's the letter B. Now tell me what letter that is?'

Jack now determined to resist, so he made no answer.

'So you cannot tell; well, then, we will try what one of these little fellows will do,' said Mr Bonnycastle, taking down a cane. 'Observe, Johnny, that's the letter B. Now, what letter is that? Answer me directly.'

'I won't learn to read and write.'

Whack came the cane on Johnny's shoulders . . .

'What letter's that?'

'I won't tell,' roared Johnny; 'I won't tell – that I won't.'

Whack – whack – whack, and a pause. 'I told you before that's the letter B. What letter is that? Tell me directly.'

Johnny, by way of reply, made snatch at the cane. Whack – he caught it, certainly; but not exactly as he would have wished. Johnny then snatched up the book and dashed it into the corner of the room. Whack, whack! Johnny attempted to seize Mr Bonnycastle with his teeth. Whack, whack, whack, whack! and Johnny fell on the carpet and roared with pain. Mr Bonnycastle then left him for a little while to recover himself, and sat down.

At last Johnny's exclamations settled down in deep sobs, and then Mr Bonnycastle said to him, 'Now, Johnny, you perceive that you must do as you are bid, or else you will have more beating. Get up immediately. Do you hear, sir?'

Somehow or another, Johnny, without intending it, stood upon his feet.

'That's a good boy; now you see, by getting up as you were bid, you have not been beaten. Now, Johnny, you must go and bring the book from where you threw it down. Do you hear, sir? Bring it directly!'

Johnny looked at Mr Bonnycastle and the cane. With every intention to refuse, Johnny picked up the book and laid it on the table.

'That's a good boy; now we will find the letter B. Here it is: now, Johnny, tell me what that letter is.'

Johnny made no answer.

'Tell me directly, sir,' said Mr Bonnycastle, raising his cane up in the air. The appeal was too powerful. Johnny eyed the cane; it moved, it was coming. Breathlessly he shrieked out, 'B.'

'Very well indeed, Johnny; very well. Now your first lesson is over, and you shall go to bed. You have learnt more than you think. To-morrow we will begin again. Now we'll put the cane by.'

* Something that cannot be done without. (Literally, in Latin: 'without which not.')

Appalling as this now sounds to us, this passage was probably originally intended to strike the reader as amusing. Today it will strike many readers as distressing – indeed, I've omitted some of the more extreme parts for that very reason. It illustrates very vividly, however, that theories and values associated with education are far from fixed. One hundred and fifty years ago – only five generations of pupils or students – this manner of 'teaching' was seen as perfectly acceptable. In fact, we don't need to go nearly as far back as that. Many teachers teaching today will have encountered corporal punishment as a part of their 'education'. Mr Bonnycastle's pupils, we are told, rather like him and see him afterwards as a friend. For us, it is hard to see him as anything but a monster engaged in the breaking of a child's will. But a hundred and fifty years ago – and less – breaking a child's will was considered by many to be a perfectly acceptable part of what education was about. However, although values change, the challenges to the teacher remain the same. We will still encounter students who don't appear to want to learn, who appear unmotivated or truculent. Of course, we find Mr Bonnycastle's solution morally repugnant. So what strategies do we, in the twenty-first century, turn to, which are consistent with our values and our professional code of conduct?

What Mr Bonnycastle is up to in this extract is behaviour modification – although he wouldn't call it by that name. He uses punishment, and the subsequent fear of punishment, to make Johnny adjust his behaviour, to bring it in line with what Mr Bonnycastle requires in a pupil. This is an approach still used by some today, in the training of animals, for example.

The feared punishment need not be physical. It might be verbal – a lot of aggressive shouting, for example. This is an approach used in the armed services. And not only in the armed services. Most of us will have experience of a teacher, manager or parent who has resorted to this approach, if not systematically, at least from time to time. The frightening thing about it, of course, is that it works. If you hurt and scare any of us enough, eventually we'll conform. But this is why we need our code of conduct, why we need to be clear about the values that attach to our professional practice; because the fact that a strategy works does not necessarily mean it's an acceptable or proper thing to do. If this were not the case we would be unable to point to the defining line between what is teaching and what is indoctrination.

Behaviour modification is based on behaviourist theories of learning. These are certainly not, however, all about using punishment, and there is a lot the teacher can usefully learn from behaviourist theories, such as how learning may be reinforced, how the learner can be motivated by achievement and reward, and so on. Some useful reading is suggested at the end of this chapter. A very different approach to encouraging student learning was advocated by Carl Rogers (1983), who suggested that students are motivated to learn through a relationship of mutual respect and trust built up between teacher and learner. To this end, argued Rogers, it is essential each learner is seen, and valued, as an individual. Essential to this teacher–student relationship is an 'unconditional positive regard' of the teacher for the learner. Having an unconditional positive regard for every one of our students is not easy, particularly when we are dealing with individuals whom we may feel to be obstructive or unkind. It does, however, represent an ideal to which we can aspire; and the motivation of students through demonstrating a respect and concern for them certainly presents us with a more positive way forward than Mr Bonnycastle's nasty methods.

But a very interesting question the behaviourist theories raise – and one which you may have identified from reading that third extract – relates to whether we can draw a distinction between education and training; and indeed whether such a distinction is useful. This debate was at its height in the 1980s, sparked by the growth of Youth Training Programmes and later by the introduction of the competence-based National Vocational Qualifications. It is a debate that is unlikely to go away, and it is one that is inevitably value-laden. Are you, for example, a teacher or a trainer? If you reply indignantly that of course you are the former, there is, implicit in your response, a value judgement that assigns a higher value or status to being a teacher. Why is this? And if you consider yourself to be a trainer, or if your role designates you as such, what is it about what you do that distinguishes you from a teacher? Is Johnny being taught by Mr Bonnycastle, or trained? When Mr Bonnycastle says to him 'You have learnt more than you think', is he talking about having taught him or having trained him? Presumably he means Johnny has not only been taught to recognise and name the letter B but has, more importantly, been trained to respond obediently to Mr Bonnycastle's command.

Close focus

An interesting way to analyse the learning which is going on in Mr Gradgrind's and Mr Bonnycastle's 'lessons' is to identify and write out what you infer to be their intended learning outcomes and their criteria for assessing whether those outcomes have been met. But whatever you do, don't muddle those up with your own lesson plans – you could be in real trouble!

You may also find it illuminating to assess these two teachers against the FENTO Standards. This will help you to familiarise yourself with the standards as well as providing a convincing argument for why such standards may be useful.

Working with others

Although our first concern is always for our students, we should not overlook the fact that our behaviour towards colleagues and others should also reflect our professionalism. The need to *respect the contribution of others to the learning process* (H2h) should always be borne in mind. What, you may ask, if I am working alongside a Mr Gradgrind? Well, that's a tricky one. But first of all let's recognise that Mr Gradgrind isn't going to be a colleague for very long, unless he changes his ways; because the Mr Gradgrinds simply won't be meeting the required FENTO Standards. Establishing a good working relationship with colleagues is important, not just for your own peace of mind at work but for the students, too. We may not approve of the way a colleague does things, but we can still behave towards him or her with the appropriate social skills of politeness and professional co-operation. Just as children will occasionally try to play Mum off against Dad or vice versa, so students will sometimes say to you: 'I wish we had you all the time. Mr Gradgrind's lessons are boring.' While this may feel very gratifying at the time, it shouldn't be encouraged. And neither should it go to your head because who knows whether they aren't saying exactly the same thing to Mr Gradgrind about you? H2c suggests we should 'Establish appropriate parameters for professional relationships' – and this is very sound advice. If you find yourself teaching with Mr Bonnycastle, on the other hand, a bit of whistle-blowing might be in order!

Engagement with your subject

A most important part of scholarship for the professional teacher is a continuing engagement with your specialist subject. There are two aspects to this: the subject itself, which may need frequent updating as in the case of information communication technology (ICT) or law; and the requirements of the curriculum and awarding bodies. These requirements have been through some rapid changes recently in many subject areas. Teachers have had, for example, to familiarise themselves and their students with several successive versions of the GNVQ specifications over the past few years. Teachers on post-16 courses have also had to get to grips with Key Skills – identifying opportunities for students to demonstrate skills in communications, application of number and IT within their specialist subject. This kind of updating is a part of continuing professional development (CPD). Sometimes it involves attending staff development courses. More frequently, it is something that has to be caught up with and digested in one's own time.

Access to the Internet makes all this very much easier. It is no coincidence that the FENTO Standards imply a basic grasp of ITC skills. The DfEE and QCA websites are valuable sources of detailed information about current developments and every awarding body has its own website now, which the teacher can access directly. Many subject specialist journals can now be accessed online; those that cannot, your college library will perhaps order for you.

Presenting the evidence

How do you present evidence your standards of professional conduct and scholarship are consistent with those described in the FENTO Standards? First of all there is your reflective journal. In Chapter 2 we focused largely on using the journal for reflecting about classroom practice, but you will also certainly find yourself using it for recording your thoughts about your specialist subject knowledge: what new developments you have read about; what questions you find yourself unable to answer and therefore need to research; and so on. Your journal will therefore contain evidence of your commitment to scholarship. The handouts and other learning materials you produce for your students will provide evidence of whether your subject knowledge is sound and up to date. Another convenient source of evidence, when you are working towards a FENTO-endorsed qualification, will be your coursework. This is almost certain to include work that demonstrates your understanding of current post-compulsory education and training (PCET) in terms of its structures and its qualifications, as well as evidence of your ability to research, process and synthesise information. Published work in academic or professional journals is, of course, another useful way of demonstrating scholarly activity.

Your commitment to working within professional codes of behaviour will be evident from your day-to-day interactions with colleagues and with students. It will be evident in your ability to be punctual for classes and to assess students' work accurately and fairly and to return it promptly. If you are a student teacher, you will demonstrate a professional attitude by putting in a full and committed day's work at the institution where you carry out your teaching practice and not taking the day off because you've missed the bus or because the budgie is poorly (I've known it happen). This evidence of your adherence to professional behaviour may be presented by your mentor, your tutor or your line manager as a written report or reference.

Your engagement with core values will be evident in all aspects of your work. For a direct source of evidence, again, your journal will be extremely useful if you have used its pages to record the ongoing debate you are sure to be having with yourself about the meaning and purpose of teaching, learning and education.

Further reading and useful websites

Reading

Ainley, P. (1993) *Class and Skill: Changing Divisions of Knowledge and Labour*. London: Cassell.

Ball, S. Maguire, M. and Macrae, S. (2000) *Choice, Pathways and Transitions Post-16*, London: Routledge Falmer.

Freire, P. (1972) *The Pedagogy of the Oppressed*. Harmondsworth: Penguin Books.

Hyland, T. (1994) *Competence, Education and NVQs: Dissenting Perspectives*. London: Cassell.

Lakoff, G. and Johnson, M. (1980) *Metaphors We Live By*. Chicago: Chicago University Press.

Maslow, A. (1987) *Motivation and Personality*. New York: Harper & Row.

Pring, R. (1995) *Closing the Gap: Liberal Education and Vocational Preparation*. London: Hodder & Stoughton.

Rogers, C. (1983) *Freedom to Learn for the 80s*. Columbus, OH: Merrill.

Rorty, R. (1989) *Contingency, Irony, and Solidarity*. Cambridge: Cambridge University Press.

Walker, S. (1984) *Learning Theory and Behaviour Modification*. London: Methuen.

Journals

Research in Post-Compulsory Education
Journal of Further and Higher Education
Vocational Aspect of Education
Education and Training

Government publications

Current white papers on education and training, as well as landmark ones such as:

DES (1986) *Working Together – Education and Training*. London: HMSO.

DfE and ED (1995) *Competitiveness – Forging Ahead: Education and Training*. London: HMSO.

DfEE (1998) *The Learning Age: A Renaissance for a New Britain*. London: HMSO.

DfEE (1999) *Learning to Succeed: A New Framework for Post-16 Learning*. London: HMSO.

DfES (2002) *Success for All: Reforming Further Education and Training*. London: DfES.

Websites

Qualifications and Curriculum Authority– www.qca.org.uk

Department for Education and Employment– www.dfee.gov.uk

Learning and Skills Development Agency – www.lsagency.org.uk

The sources

The first extract was from Charles Dickens' *Hard Times* (1854). The second was from Plato's *Republic* (c. 370–390 BC). The third was from Captain Marryat's *Mr Midshipman Easy* (1836).

9 THE MINIMUM CORE AND KEY SKILLS

This chapter examines the important role the Minimum Core plays in the day-to-day professional practice of teaching and supporting learning, and in enabling the FE teacher to support learners' development of Key Skills. It also explains how Key Skills have come to occupy a central position in the post-14 curriculum and looks at some of the issues teachers and learners have raised in relation to them. It includes some examples and exercises which will enable the teacher to evaluate their own key skills against what is demanded by their teaching. This ability to so evaluate is explicitly referred to in the Minimum Core specifications (www.lifelonglearninguk.org) and in the following areas of skills and knowledge.

→ **Introduction stage**
Skills: D2i, D3a, D3b, D3c, G3a

→ **Intermediate stage**. All the above, plus
Skills: C2f, D2h, D3d, D3f, D5e, D5g, D5j, E3c, G1f

→ **Certification stage.** All the above, plus
Skills: A1c, A2b, B1f

→ **Essential knowledge.** Specifically areas listed under
a2, b1, b2, b3, d2, d3, d5, e3, g3

Why the Minimum Core?

The Minimum Core refers to a set of skills and underlying theory in literacy, language and numeracy introduced by FENTO in August 2003 and fully implemented as an integral part of FE teacher training programmes from September 2004. The introduction of the Core was a strategy to ensure that all trainee FE teachers are themselves equipped to support learners' development of appropriate Key Skills (see below). The teacher's ability to assess and develop students' competence in the Key Skills, particularly in Communication, is implicit throughout the National Standards. The teacher's grasp of the Minimum Core – and particularly the language and literacy elements of it on which this chapter focuses – is essential to this process. Section GI of the National Standards requires that FE teachers will be able to 'evaluate their own key skills against what is required in their teaching'. The purpose of the Minimum Core is to provide a set of criteria against which they can do this.

So, what do we mean by Key Skills? The Key Skills with which this chapter is particularly concerned are those currently offered for assessment and accreditation as the Key Skills Qualification, which is a part of Curriculum 2000. They are

Communication, Information Technology (IT) and Application of Number. It is important to be clear about this because the title 'key skills' can be confusing. Before 1996, the term more commonly used was 'core skills'. Organisations and initiatives, such as the NCVQ, BTEC and the Technical and Vocational Education Initiative (TVEI), had their own descriptors for these core skills, but the skills themselves were broadly the same. This was because they had a common ancestor.

In 1974 Jim Callaghan, then prime minister, raised the issue of core skills in his famous Ruskin Speech, arguing that young people were leaving school without the skills employers required of them. But Key Skills, as we understand them today, can be traced back to a document produced by the Further Education Unit (FEU) in 1979, entitled *A Basis for Choice* – sometimes referred to in shorthand as ABC. This advocated a core entitlement for all students in FE, which would include awareness of the economy and the world of work, as well as communication, numeracy and personal skills. It was influential in shaping some of the innovative and interesting aspects of, for example, BTEC courses in the 1980s. Its influence can certainly be seen in the content of the 'off-the-job' component of the Youth Training Scheme (YTS), in the form of 'Social and Life Skills'.

In 1990 the National Curriculum Council (NCC) listed six core skill areas. These were communication, problem-solving, personal skills, numeracy, IT and a modern foreign language. These corresponded with the core skills listed at the same time by TVEI. The emphasis was still upon the argument that these were the skills employers wanted young people to have. In the same year there was a recommendation (from SEAC) that core skills should become a compulsory part of the A-level curriculum. This was presented as a way of broadening the curriculum whilst at the same time leaving traditional A-levels relatively untouched. When Sir Ron Dearing presented his review of 16–19 qualifications in 1996, he included a similar proposal. Identifying core skills as one of the strengths of the GNVQ curriculum, he recommended the same skills be required across all 16–19 qualifications. In the report they are referred to as Key Skills and this terminology has stuck. We no longer speak of core skills but of Key Skills, although we are referring to what are fundamentally the same areas of achievement.

The inclusion of Key Skills as an optional component of Curriculum 2000 can be traced back to Dearing's recommendation. We now have six Key Skills, still recognisable as descendants from those listed in *A Basis for Choice*, although, of course, the skills related to IT assume much more importance now than they did a quarter of a century ago. They are:

1. Communication.
2. IT.
3. Application of Number.
4. Working with Others.
5. Improving own Learning and Performance.
6. Problem-solving.

These also form a central part of Modern Apprenticeships. Recognition is given to all six, but only three are externally assessed. These are the Big Three: Communication, IT and Application of Number, and they are the same skills which, FENTO suggests, are essential for the FE teacher.

We've lost some core/key skills on the way. A modern foreign language, for example, is not included in the current Key Skills nor are two of those originally suggested in Callaghan's Ruskin speech: 'respect for others' and 'respect for the individual'. These last two have metamorphosed, perhaps, into the current 'Working with Others'.

Key Skills and Curriculum 2000

Although the Key Skills Qualification is not at the moment a mandatory part of Curriculum 2000, many students will now be developing Key Skills as part of their post-16 studies. This means that their teachers, too, whatever their subject, will need to be confident they can support and assess students in these aspects of their work. The development and assessment of all three so-called 'hard' key skills takes place within the post-16 curriculum context of A-levels (A2), AS-levels and AVCEs, as well as Modern Apprenticeships. At this level, students are expected to achieve Level 3 Key Skills. Those studying at Intermediate level are expected to achieve Key Skills at Level 2. Most teachers in FE will find themselves teaching at both these levels. There is a clear need, therefore, for teachers themselves to ensure they are competent in these areas. Hence the introduction of the Minimum Core, which in addition encourages understanding of the ways in which language and literacy skills can impact on the learners' ability to learn, and indeed on their ability to participate constructively in society as a whole.

Some might argue this is not necessary because Key Skills are not fully integrated into the curriculum at their particular college but are the domain of specialist teachers in separately timetabled sessions. However, this issue is not simply about the teaching and assessment of Key Skills but about how we model these skills for our students.

Task

Look at the following list of activities and interactions which provides examples of where the teacher's implementation of Minimum Core skills may be used to model good practice for the development of learners' Key Skills.

a) Identify those which are relevant to your own practice.

b) List any additional activities and/or interactions (e.g. in Numeracy) where you think the Minimum Core fulfils this purpose.

Communication
- Speaking to students as individuals and as groups.
- Listening to students as individuals and as groups.
- Writing on the board, flipchart, OHP.
- Pre-preparing handouts and other learning materials.
- Giving clear explanations.
- Summarising information.

- Using language appropriate to your audience.
- Using language appropriate to the situation.
- Spelling, punctuating and pronouncing correctly.

Application of Number
- Calculating marks correctly.
- Dividing students into small groups efficiently.
- Calculating the correct number of resources needed for the group.
- Being confident and competent in making calculations related to your subject.
- Being able to handle statistical information correctly (e.g. in social sciences).

Information Technology
- Producing learning materials.
- Using the Internet as a resource.
- Using IT in presentations (e.g. PowerPoint).
- Contacting students by email.
- Advising students on presentation of work (spell-check, format, etc.).
- Receiving and assessing student work submitted electronically.
- Keeping up to date in your subject area by using the Internet.

Key Skills-related activities

Of these three, Application of Number is often seen as the most problematic. It isn't always easy to see where we use it in our professional practice and, during the early days of GNVQs, it was the key/core skill most likely to be handled separately by a specialist teacher. But if we look at the current DfEE guidelines we see that students who have a GCSE in maths, grade A–C, are exempt from the Level 2 external assessment in number. This level of numeracy should not be daunting even for the teacher who is not a maths specialist. From a professional point of view it is interesting to bear in mind that teachers entering the primary sector are now required to undergo testing in literacy and numeracy skills.

Key Skills, basic skills and study skills

Reference is made to all three of these in the FENTO Standards, and it is important they are not confused because they relate to very different student needs and achievements. The Key Skills, as we have seen, are a part of the post-16 curriculum. The Key Skills Qualification gives UCAS points which may be counted towards the entry requirement for HE and certifies that the student possesses those skills – Communication, Number and IT – employers find desirable in first-time applicants. Basic skills, on the other hand, usually refer to the skills of reading, writing, speaking and number which some students, having left compulsory schooling, are still not confident about. There are a variety of reasons why students may need tuition in basic skills. A learning difficulty, an unsettled pattern of schooling or frequent non-attendance may have set up a barrier to their learning. Or it may have been a matter of motivation. Teaching in basic skills may have its own timetable and take place one to one, with teachers working with individual students or as small or large group workshops. Or it may be linked to learning support, where students who need it are supported in their general or vocational classes by a specialist basic-skills teacher.

Study skills are a third category, related in some ways but significantly different in others. They are, as the name suggests, the skills students need to have in order to be able to work effectively as independent learners. They include, for example, the ability to take clear, relevant and adequate notes; to find information both from libraries and from electronic sources; and to plan and utilise time efficiently.

As teachers, our function in relation to these three types of skills is likely to be different in each case. We should all be able to model competence in the Key Skills for our students and help them to develop their own, although we will not necessarily be formally teaching or assessing all or any of them. The teaching of basic skills is sometimes a specialist role, often requiring specialist training, but as teachers we need to be able to identify where our students might need help with basic skills and to ensure they receive the appropriate, specialist support if necessary. We should all, however, think of ourselves as teachers of study skills. In order that our students receive the help and guidance they need in note-taking, time management and research skills, we need to build opportunities for this into our lesson plans and schemes of work, because this is one of the ways in which we will encourage our students to become effective and independent learners.

What student teachers have to say about Key Skills and the Minimum Core

It is interesting to look at what a group of student teachers in FE have to say about the Key Skills at the outset of their Certification stage programme. Very few expressed concerns about Number, perhaps because it was a requirement for their programme that they should have at least a GCSE A-C or equivalent in maths, and so they felt reasonably well equipped to cope with that particular skill. Information Technology, however, was another matter. Here are some of the things they said:

> 'I've never come into contact with a computer – I've always avoided it.'
> 'I've only ever used IT to type up my dissertation.'
> 'Apart from word processing and accessing the Internet, I'm a novice.'

After eight months, towards the end of their second block of teaching practice, these same student teachers were using IT to produce handouts, prepare presentations and set up learning sites on their host college's intranet. The moral here is that, given the proper guidance, anyone can – and should – do it.

Student teachers' concerns over Communication are often very specific and centre upon anxiety about the possibility of making mistakes in spelling and punctuation, especially when writing, unprepared, on a flipchart or board:

> 'There are some words I've just got a blind spot about. I'm not going to write them here, because I'll get them wrong! But I have a horror of students putting their hands up and saying, "Hey, that's not how you spell that".'

'Apostrophes. We never did apostrophes at school. Usually I just get around it by leaving them out. But I'm not going to be able to do that on handouts and things. I've got to get to grips with it now, because otherwise how will I help students get it right?'

In confessing to their fears and their blind spots, all these student teachers are doing something very important in terms of their professional practice. Skill G1f in the FENTO Standards requires that teachers should 'Evaluate their own key skills against what is required in their teaching'. In doing just this, these student teachers are taking the first step towards updating and improving their own skills. This is what the Minimum Core is designed to equip the teacher to do.

Task

Evaluate this handout in terms of how good a model the teacher is providing of competence in Key Skills.

Intermediate Buisness

As you watch the video during todays' lesson, look out for and write down the answers to the following. Just the bear facts will do.

1. Can the Trading Standards Office act on it' s own initiative?

2. Can a company compare there own product with the product of a named competitor?

3. What is the ASA and what does it do?

4. What legal constraint's are imposed on the promotion (advertising) of cigarette's?

5. Who should the public complain to if their holiday accomodation does'nt match that advertised in the brochure?

Intermediate Business handout

Clearly the handout is an example of what happens when a teacher is not taking sufficient care to provide his or her students with a good model of Communication Key Skills. The layout is easy on the eye because it has made use of a large font and careful spacing. To this extent, it demonstrates skill in IT. But what about the spelling? There are mistakes here that a spellcheck would have corrected – although there are others which would probably not be picked up electronically, being incorrect only in context. The punctuation leaves much to be desired. (We might even wish this teacher had read, despite all its disadvantages, the handout on apostrophes we looked at in Chapter 7.) If you'd like to proofread and correct it – which is what the student teacher who produced it should have done – you'll find the corrected version at the end of this chapter.

Task

Now read through this redrafted version of the apostrophe handout we looked at in Chapter 7. Are there any further improvements you could suggest?

Communication Key Skills Level 3
Apostrophes

The rules for using apostrophes are very simple. They are as follows:

1. Using the apostrophe to show that something belongs to somebody
The apostrophe always attaches to the end of the owner or owners.
So, if the bowl belongs to the dog, it is the dog's bowl.
If the hat belongs to the man, it is the man's hat.
If the bowl belongs to several dogs who have to share it, it is the dogs' bowl.
We don't put another 's' on the end of dogs' simply because it would become too
    much of a mouthful to say. It would sound something like, 'the dogzizz bowl'.
If several men had to share one hat (an unlikely situation, certainly), we would have
    to call it the men's hat.
So that is the rule. The apostrophe attaches to the end of whoever is the owner or
owners. Now you try.

The beard of the man becomes . . . .
The glare of the sun becomes. . . . .
The end of the year becomes . . . .
The games of the children become . . . .
The wool of the one sheep becomes . . . .
The wool of several sheep becomes. . . . .

2. Using the apostrophe to show that something is missing.

It is easy to remember this rule if you think of the apostrophe as a sort of wedge
holding open the gap where one letter or more is missing.

So, for example, when we abbreviate I am to I'm, the apostrophe shows us where a
letter (in this case the 'a' from 'am') is missing.

When we abbreviate is not to isn't, the apostrophe shows us where the 'o' used to
be.
When we abbreviate it is to it's, the apostrophe shows us where the 'i' used to be.
And do remember, it's always and only means 'it is' or 'it has'.

It's that simple. There is never any reason to get it wrong.

NB The apostrophe in o'clock is there because the full phrase was originally of the
clock. The apostrophe marks the place where the 'f ' and the 'the' used to be.
So now try using apostrophes to abbreviate the following:

You are   He is

I am not   What is going on?

Where is it gone?   How is Dad?

It is a nice day, is it not? [literally: is not it?]

What about some of the stray apostrophes we encounter here and there?

You may have seen market stalls advertising GRANNY SMITH'S 1.20/kilo. This is a rogue apostrophe. Whoever wrote the notice has got it wrong. Go and ask them, 'Granny Smith's what?'

You may have seen, even in respectable literature, references to GNVQ's. This apostrophe is not strictly wrong; but it is quite unnecessary. No letters are missing; no ownership is being indicated; but there is a tradition in English for using apostrophes when making a plural of numbers (e.g. 1880's) or initial letters. However, this can confuse the issue, and GNVQs is a perfectly correct usage in the 2000s.

Task

If your own grasp of apostrophes is shaky, have a go at the exercises on the handout. They will give you an indication of whether you are meeting this aspect of the Level 3 Key Skills requirement in Communication. The correct answers can be found at the end of this chapter.

Close focus

Is that an improvement, do you think? Is there anything you would still like to change? Does the handout encourage independent learning, for example? Do the exercises give enough practice and cover a sufficient range? What about the length? Do you think the material should be divided between two handouts, perhaps, rather than given out all as one? If so, what would your argument be for this?

We should never lose sight of the fact that one of our roles, as a teacher, is to model good practice. This doesn't mean we have to know everything but it may certainly mean setting a standard for social skills and interaction or presenting ourselves as an example of enthusiasm and conscientiousness. And it always involves modelling correct spelling and punctuation. This is one of the reasons why FENTO make frequent reference to clear communication in the standards. Students will assume the way you spell something or punctuate something is the right way because you are their teacher. And they will copy you. So if you're not sure about the spelling of *accommodation, occasionally, separate,* or *definitely* – or whatever happens to be your blind spot – don't pass that error on to students but use your spellcheck and get someone to proofread your handouts as well for good measure.

Further reading and useful websites

Reading

Callaghan, J. (1976) Towards a national debate (text of the Ruskin speech), *Education*, 22, pp. 332-33.

Dearing, R. (1996) *Review of Qualifications for 16–19-Year-olds.* London: SCAA.

Munday, F. and Faraday, S. (1999) *Key Skills: Strategies in Action.* London: FEDA.

Websites

www. lifelonglearninguk.org/documents/svukdocs/minimumcore

Qualifications and Curriculum Authority – www.qca.org.uk

Key Skills support programme – www.keyskillssupport.net

Awarding bodies for Key Skills qualifications – www.aqa.org.uk; www. asdan.co.uk; www.city-and-guilds.co.uk; www.ocr.org.uk

Answers

If you had a go at the exercises, here are the correct answers for you to check against your own.

The beard of the man becomes: The man's beard.

The glare of the sun becomes: The sun's glare.

The end of the year becomes: The year's end.

The games of the children become: The children's games.

The wool of the one sheep becomes: One sheep's wool.

The wool of several sheep becomes: Several sheep's wool (because the plural of sheep is still sheep).

You are = you're.

He is = he's.

I am not = I'm not.

What is going on? = What's going on?

Where is it gone? = Where's it gone?

How is Dad? = How's Dad?

It is a nice day, is it not? = It's a nice day, isn't it?

And here, just for the record, are the corrections for the mistakes you will have noticed in the business studies handout at the beginning of this task.

GNVQ Intermediate Business

As you watch the video during today's lesson, look out for and write down the answers to the following. Just the bare facts will do.

1. Can the Trading Standards Office act on its own initiative?
2. Can a company compare their own product with the product of a named competitor?
3. What is the ASA and what does it do?
4. What legal constraints are imposed on the promotion (advertising) of cigarettes?
5. Whom should the public complain to if their holiday accommodation doesn't match that advertised in the brochure?

This chapter sets out a range of currently accepted theories of learning and relates them to familiar classroom situations. It goes on to explain how teachers themselves can set about theorising, based on their own experience. The material in this chapter may be used for developing and reinforcing the following areas of skills and knowledge as set out in the National Occupational (FENTO) Standards:

→ **d1, d2, d3, d4, e4, f2, g1, g2, g3, h1, h2**

The relevance of theories of learning

What do we mean when we use the term Theories of Learning? Broadly speaking, we are talking about how people learn and about what factors are likely to help them to learn best. From a teacher's point of view, the important thing about theories of learning is their practical application. In the classroom or the workshop a theory is only useful if it works. In this chapter we look at a range of learning theories, and in each example you are encouraged to ask yourself:

● Is this true in my experience?

● Can I think of examples from my own experience which illustrate this theory in action?

● Can I usefully apply this to my own professional practice?

In the past, Theories of Learning came under the general heading of Psychology of Education. This is a vast field. The small corner of it we'll be looking at here focuses on this issue.

● What motivates people to learn?

Or, to put it another way ...

● Under what conditions do people learn best?

These two questions are ones which a good teacher will always continue to explore and reflect on, however long they have been in the business. At the end of this chapter you'll find a list of suggested reading which will allow you to explore in more depth some of the ideas briefly set out here.

Broadly speaking, we can divide Learning Theory into three schools of thought: The Behaviourists, the Cognitivists, and the Humanists. We'll take each one of those in turn and look at what they mean in terms of classroom practice.

The Behaviourists

When people think of Behaviourists they tend to picture someone in a white coat teaching tricks to laboratory animals, or inducing neurosis in small children by frightening them with loud noises. Not only does this give the Behaviourist theories a bad press, it makes some teachers wonder how this work can possibly have any relevance for their own professional practice. The reality, however, is that the Behaviourist model can be a very useful one for understanding what motivates students to comply, to cooperate and to learn. The two most famous names associated with Behaviourism are Watson and Skinner. At its most straightforward their work has been taken to mean that we can be motivated to learn by reward, and that by 'reward' we might mean something as basic as the avoidance of pain. In other words, the consequences of our actions or responses – rewarding or painful – can lead us to change, repeat or give up those actions or responses. For example, if you find you are praised for attempting to answer a question, even if you get it wrong, you'll be even more inclined to risk offering an answer next time too. If, however, your teacher's response to a wrong answer is withering sarcasm or a disapproving 'No!' you'll probably not feel like sticking your neck out the next time. In these circumstances, praise from the teacher would be called, in Behaviourist terms, *positive reinforcement*. Positive reinforcement can be any response that makes the recipient feel so good that they're likely to repeat the same behaviour next time the opportunity arises so that they will come in for that same reward. The teacher could have given sweets. They could even have given five-pound notes. But praise will work just as well and it's easier on the pocket!

It's important to remember, however, that the same dynamic can work in a less obvious and less positive way too. Imagine that, instead of putting up your hand to offer an answer (or shouting it out if you want to be less formal about it), you get up and wander about the classroom, distracting other learners and generally making a nuisance of yourself. This may very well get you lots of attention from the teacher, albeit of a disapproving kind. Nevertheless, you may well feel that disapproval is better than no attention at all. You may even feel that disapproval is the only kind of attention that you can ever realistically hope for, so you'll take it, thank you very much. In this situation the pay-off is having the teacher's attention at all. Being told repeatedly to sit down and be quiet is the positive reinforcement which perpetuates that very behaviour.

In other words, the Behaviourist model can be useful to draw upon when we reflect on how our responses as teachers to our students' behaviour can affect that behaviour in the future. Although, of course, we must ensure that our responses are consistent.

The Cognitivists

In Chapter 6 of this book we talked about the three domains of learning: Cognitive, Affective and Psychomotor. Cognitive, you remember, is to do with thinking; and so, as you might expect, the Cognitivist theory of learning argues that *thinking* is central to the learning process. In other words, it argues that learning is about much more than the modification of behaviour through positive or negative reinforcement. It is about the learner gaining progressively more and newer knowledge, while at the same time adapting or discarding old knowledge which no longer fits their growing insight into the world. From the teacher's point of view this has important implications for the structuring and planning of lessons. The most important is that these should provide learning opportunities which will develop the students' understanding and allow them to explore the relationships between ideas and concepts, rather than, for example, simply learning to recite the bare facts about them.

The Humanists

We've already mentioned two major theorists of the Humanist school, although we haven't identified them with that label: Abraham Maslow (page 92) and Carl Rogers (pages 115-116). The Humanists are often regarded as being somehow in opposition to the Behaviourists. Indeed, their school of thought grew to some extent out of resistance to Behaviourist thinking, which was seen as mechanistic and dehumanising. For the Humanists the important issue is the essential dignity and self-worth of every individual, and the potential of every individual to achieve, in Maslow's term, *self-actualisation*.

However, to view the Behaviourist and Humanist theories as an either/or choice would be to throw away much that is useful. Taken together, they offer the teacher a range of possible strategies and responses to try out depending on the circumstances and the situation. Undeniably there are contradictions. Faced with a disruptive student, for example, a Behaviourist might caution: 'Ignore her. Any attention you give her will amount to *positive reinforcement*. She'll take it as a reward and keep on repeating the behaviour'. The Rogers-inspired Humanist, however, could well advise: 'Despite this learner's disruptive behaviour, she still deserves your *unconditional positive regard*. How can you possibly ignore her?' And the Humanist inspired by Maslow would probably say: 'This learner can't learn *until her basic needs are met*. Perhaps she is afraid. Perhaps she fears that if she actually sits down and tries to apply herself to the task you've set her, she won't be able to do it and will lose what little self-esteem she has'.

Which path to choose? You are the teacher. Part of what it means to be a professional is to take the responsibility to weigh up the situation, draw on your theoretical knowledge, and make a choice.

Propositional knowledge

In working through these summaries of the key areas of learning theory you will no doubt have been relating them in your mind's eye to your own experiences in the classroom, as teacher or learner or both. It's likely that some aspects of theory will ring truer for you than others. What is most important to remember is that, however famous a theory might be, if it doesn't work in practice then it's not much use to you. One of the many advantages of keeping a reflective journal is that you are able to review and analyse your own experience, and from this to build your own accumulation of knowledge – knowledge derived from trying out different ways of doing things, and seeing what works. In doing this you are inevitably coming up with your own theories about how and why people learn. You are theorising. Part of the mark of a true professional is that you will continue learning and theorising and adapting those theories in the light of your experience (do you spot the Cognitivist model there?) for as long as you call yourself a Teacher.

Further reading

A detailed account of the theories of learning mentioned here can be found in:

Curzon, L. B. (1997) *Teaching in Further Education*. London: Cassell (Fifth Edition).

If you'd like to go to the original source, two fairly readable suggestions are:

Maslow, A. (1987) *Motivation and Personality*. New York: Harper and Row.
Rogers, C. (1983) *Freedom to Learn for the 80s*. Columbus, OH: Merrill.

And an oldish but entertaining account of Behaviourist theory:

Walker, S. (1984) *Learning Theory and Behaviour Modification*. London: Methuen.

For an account of these theories in action:

Wallace, S. (2002) *Managing Behaviour and Motivating Students in Further Education*. Exeter: Learning Matters.

11 FORMS AND FORMALITIES: GUIDANCE AND EXEMPLAR MATERIAL

This chapter provides examples of documentation that can be used for mapping and recording the ways in which you demonstrate that your practice reflects the FENTO Standards. These are for illustrative purposes and references made in them to specific skills apply to the Introduction stage only. These can be easily expanded to cover the other stages. The cross-referencing to be found in the Appendix makes this quite straightforward. This chapter is relevant, therefore, to all skill areas at all three stages.

The observer's evaluation of your lesson

The observer may be your mentor, tutor or quality manager. At the Introduction stage the evaluation of the lesson should cover at least those aspects of the teaching and learning that provide opportunities for the teacher to demonstrate the following skills: B2e, D1b, H1d, C2e, H1f and Key Skills. In addition, they may make reference to such of the other skills or areas of knowledge as the observer deems to be relevant, such as those specifically referred to in your action plan. The evaluation could be presented in this format.

Teacher's name: **Date:**

Observer's name: **No. in class:**

Subject, topic, and level:

....

....

....

Does the teacher create a safe, productive learning environment based on mutual trust and if so, how? [B2e/D1b/H1d]

....

....

....

How does the teacher ensure that all students are involved in the learning activities? [c2e]

....

....

....

How does the teacher promote equality of opportunity and address the needs of all learners? [H1f]

....

....

....

How does the teacher demonstrate and develop the Key Skills of communication, IT, and Application of Number?

....

....

....

Additional comment:
Planning and assessment

....
....
....

Teaching

....
....

Learning

....
....

Resources

....
....
....

The teacher has provided the following documentation

Lesson plan ☐

Rationale and action plan ☐

A copy of this evaluation; was given to the teacher and discussed fully on .... (date)

Signature of observer ....

Signature of teacher ....

Observer's evaluation

The rationale for the lesson plan

This is your opportunity to explain how and why the lesson has been planned as it has. At the Introductory stage it could be set out using the following headings :

1. 'How the content relates to, and has been extrapolated from, the specifications or syllabus' [B1d].
2. 'How the characteristics of these particular learners have been taken into account when planning the lesson' [A1a, H1b, H1k, H1f].
3. 'How the activities and resources have been designed to engage and motivate the learners' [B2a, D5f].
4. 'How the assessment methods meet the criteria of validity, reliability, fairness and coherence, as well as meeting the needs of the learners' [A2a, F1a, F1b, F1c, F1e, F1g].
5. 'How opportunities are used to develop learners' Key Skills and study skills' [D2i, D2j].
6. 'How learners are encouraged to take responsibility for their own learning' [E2e].
7. 'How the teacher's own practice will promote equality of opportunity' [H1f].
8. 'How the teacher's own experience of learning has informed the planning of the lesson' [H1h].
9. 'How best use will be made of resources, under existing constraints' [H2i].

Subject / level _____ Group _____ Date _____ Duration _____ No of students _____

Time	Content	Outcomes	Method	Student activity	Assessment	Key skills	Resources

Strategies / opportunities for supporting learners with specific needs:

Suggested format for a lesson plan

Your own evaluation of the lesson

After the planned lesson has been taught, the teacher should produce a written evaluation of that lesson which demonstrates his or her ability to reflect constructively upon his or her professional practice. This could be produced informally, as part of the reflective journal, or as a formal evaluation submitted to the tutor, mentor or whoever was responsible for observing the lesson.

In the light of these reflections, the teacher may choose to make revisions to the original lesson plan for future use. At the Introduction stage the evaluation could be set out using the following headings:

1. How effective was the learning? [C1g, C2g, C3h].
2. How were individual learners' needs met? [H1k].
3. How might the lesson plan be modified/revised for future use? [C2g, C3h, G1i].
4. How appropriate and effective were the teaching and learning materials and resources used? [D5f].
5. How did the teacher ensure he or she had feedback in order to help measure the quality of the teaching and learning? [D7c].
6. How it was ensured that learners understood the purpose and nature of the assessment process' [F1d].
7. How was assessment information used to judge how the learning objectives had been achieved? [F2b].
8. How was assessment information used in evaluating own performance as a teacher? [F2c, G1i].
9. Based on assessment information gathered in the lesson, how might the teaching be improved? [F2d, G1i, G3a].

The witness statement

The witness statement should be completed, signed and dated by the teacher's mentor/tutor/quality manager. At the Introductory stage it could be set out under the following headings:

1. [B3b] 'The teacher maintains effective links with the following agencies in the following ways to enhance curriculum delivery:'

    ....

2. [B3d] 'The teacher's support for a culture of open access and widening participation is demonstrated by:'

    ....

3. [E3d] 'Examples of the ways in which the teacher liaises with colleagues and other professionals to provide the most effective guidance and support for learners are as follows:'

    ....

4. [H2b] 'The teacher maintains a professional form of behaviour towards learners and others. This is evident from:'

....

5. [H2d] 'The teacher's responsibility for the effectiveness of education and training and a commitment to the well-being, progress and achievement of learners is demonstrated by:'

....

6. [H2e] 'The teacher is aware of and meets his or her personal responsibility to learners and others within the framework of the organisation's rules, regulations and duties of care towards learners and others. For example:'

....

7. [H2h] 'The teacher respects the contribution of others to the learning process. For example:'

....

Observing an experienced practitioner

You should take every opportunity to observe experienced and qualified practitioners as they teach and support student learning. To make the most of these learning opportunities, it is useful to record your observations. The following format suggests one way in which this can be done systematically.

Subject/level/year: ....

No. of students: ....

1. Layout of room (draw diagram if appropriate)

2. Student characteristics (age, gender, behaviour, etc.)

3. Methods and strategies (and how these relate to 1 and 2)

4. Patterns and styles of communication (teacher–students/students–students) and how this relates to 1, 2 and 3.

5. How material was sequenced, presented and made accessible (relate to 2, 3 and 4)

6. Critical incidents – how they arose and how they were dealt with.

APPENDIX: MAPPING YOUR TEACHING AND LEARNING ACTIVITIES AGAINST THE FENTO STANDARDS

In this appendix you will find suggested teaching and learning activities appropriate to each of the skills and essential areas of knowledge listed in the FENTO Standards. These activities and potential sources of evidence are presented in three stages, appropriate to the Introduction, the Intermediate and the Certification stages of a teaching and learning qualification in FE. Where there is a close correspondence between skills from different key areas, reference to the related skills is made in brackets. For example, there is a close correspondence between A1a ('*Acknowledge the previous learning experiences and achievements of learners*') and H1b ('*Acknowledge the diversity of learners' experience and support the development needs of individuals*'). In such cases, the evidence requirements will be closely related.

The core activity for the Introduction stage is the planning, justification, implementation and evaluation of a lesson or series of lessons that are observed and assessed, or recorded and assessed, by a tutor or mentor. This could include a video-taped micro-teach of about ten minutes' duration, delivered to colleagues or other student teachers. The benefits of this particular activity are that the teacher is able to review and evaluate his or her performance and to refer to it over time as a measure of how far he or she has progressed in skills and confidence.

The activities and knowledge appropriate to the two subsequent stages build upon this core activity and reflect the teacher's expanding scope and experience. If carefully documented, they will generate the evidence required to demonstrate the teacher has the skills and knowledge appropriate to his or her stage of the qualification. Suggestions for ways in which this evidence may be collected for assessment purposes are to be found in Chapter 10.

The final section of this appendix takes a different approach, this time taking the suggested evidence as the starting point and mapping this against the standards. This also serves to illustrate again where there is close correspondence between skills from different key areas and shows, therefore, how several skills can be addressed or demonstrated through the same teaching and learning activity.

The Introduction stage: defining the evidence

In the mapping grid for the Introduction stage which follows, you will find various sources of evidence suggested. Some of these will be documents that will be generated naturally in the course of good professional practice. These include, for example, lesson plans and resources such as handouts, ICT material or OHTs. Some of the evidence will be generated by the fact you are working towards a teaching qualification. For example, you will have evaluative reports about your teaching, written by the tutor or mentor who has observed your lesson, and you will be producing your own reflective evaluation of your practice in the form of a reflective journal or written lesson evaluations.

Let's look carefully, then, at exactly what these pieces of evidence, which are referred to in the grid below, entail.

A video-taped record of a lesson or series of lessons

A video-recording of yourself teaching is one of the most useful resources you can have in terms of reflecting upon and developing your own practice. You may choose to have a record of a full session of teaching and learning with your students, or you may prefer to video a micro-teaching session of ten or fifteen minutes where you are teaching colleagues or fellow student teachers as a part of your teacher education programme. Whichever you choose, the advantage of such a recording is that you can view and review it on your own in order to get a student's-eye view of yourself as teacher and, at the same time, make a professional appraisal of your own strengths and weaknesses. This makes an excellent starting point for putting together your action plan for professional development. If you keep the tape safe, you can make a second recording after some weeks or months have elapsed so that, watching the two in sequence, you can judge to what extent aspects of your practice have developed or improved. For the purposes of evidence, of course, a video-tape of your teaching is very useful indeed, particularly if it provides a record of sessions for which you also have documentation of planning, resources and evaluation.

A detailed lesson plan for the lesson(s)

You will find guidance on the writing of lessons' plans in Chapter 3, and suggested lesson plan templates in Chapter 10.

A written evaluation of the lesson(s) by your mentor, tutor or manager

This is the evaluation produced by whoever has observed and/or assessed your teaching. If you are a student teacher you will receive these as a matter of course. If you are already employed as a teacher and are working towards a teaching qualification, you may be able to use written feedback arising from peer evaluation or staff development assessments arising from your college's self-assessment activity. Some suggested formats for feedback can be found in Chapter 10.

A written rationale for the lesson plan

You may be required to produce rationales for your lesson plans as a part of your teacher training programme. These may be included in your reflective journal or documented separately and formally for the purposes of assessment. A rationale or justification does just what its name suggests. It explains why you are teaching these particular students this particular topic in this particular way. You will find further guidance and a suggested format in Chapter 10.

Your own evaluation of the lesson(s)

This is the evaluation you produce after you have planned and taught the lesson. How did it go? This may be something you confine to your journal or you may be required to produce a separate, formal evaluation as part of the coursework required for your qualification. Guidelines and format can be found in Chapter 10.

Teaching and learning materials

It is important that some of these should be of your own design, if you are to demonstrate the full range of skills. You should also be able to produce learning materials using the Internet as a resource, as this not only demonstrates your own ICT skills but also encourages your students to use electronic sources of information.

A reflective journal

Guidance for keeping the journal is given in Chapter 2. Extracts covering the period during which the planning, teaching and evaluation were taking place may prove a useful source of evidence.

Copies of relevant documentation

A useful source of evidence would be the various kinds of institutional documentation you may have completed as part of this period of professional practice. This could include, for example, copies of attendance lists or resource booking forms.

A witness statement from your mentor/tutor/ manager

It is unlikely you can capture every aspect of your teaching and learning activities on video-tape or produce evidence from naturally occurring documentation. It may be useful, therefore, to have a written account from an appropriate witness confirming you carry out your professional activities to the required standard. You will find suggested formats for presenting witness statements in Chapter 10.

Where you have demonstrated skills in your teaching, your evidence after the event will consist of any or all of the following: the video-tape, the observer's evaluation, student feedback, a witness statement.

Mapping grid: Introduction stage

	Skill	Suggested evidence
A1a	Acknowledge the previous learning experiences and achievements of learners (H1b)	• rationale for lesson plan • journal • video • tutor/mentor evaluation
A2a	Consider and apply a range of assessment techniques	• rationale • plan • video • tutor/mentor evaluation
A2h	Provide feedback to the learner in the outcome of the assessment and its consequences	• video • tutor/mentor evaluation
B1a	Interpret curriculum requirements in terms of syllabuses, objectives and schemes of work for learning programmes.	• lesson plans and/or scheme of work
B1c	Establish precise learning objectives and content	• lesson plans and/or scheme of work
B1d	Define the subject knowledge, technical knowledge and skills required	• lesson plans • rationales
B2a	Encourage learners to adopt styles of learning that are appropriate to the required outcomes and most likely to enable learners to achieve to the best of their abilities	• lesson plans • rationales
B2e	Create a safe learning environment based on trust and support (H1d) (see D1b)	• video • tutor/mentor evaluation
B3b	Maintain effective links with appropriate agencies to enhance curriculum delivery	• witness statement with examples
B3d	Support a culture of open access and widening participation	• witness statement with examples
C1d	Identify and produce appropriate video/tutor/mentor evaluation and learning materials that engage learners' interest and reinforce their learning (see C2f)	• teaching and learning materials
C1g	Evaluate the effectiveness of learning (see C2g)	• your evaluation of lesson • journal
C2b	Produce learning plans that encourage learning in groups	• lesson plan
C2e	Ensure that all members of the group are involved in learning activities	• video • tutor/mentor evaluation
C2f	Produce appropriate learning support materials using ICT where appropriate (see C1d)	• teaching and learning materials
C2g	Evaluate the effectiveness of learning and modify teaching plans where necessary (see C3h, C2g)	• your evaluation of lesson • journal • redrafted lesson plan
C3f	Support learners as they learn	• video • tutor/mentor evaluation
C3h	Evaluate effectiveness of the learning process and modify teaching plans where necessary	• your evaluation of lesson • journal • redrafted lesson plan
D1b	Ensure an interactive, safe and productive learning environment that fosters learners' security and confidence	• video • tutor/mentor evaluation

D1c	Maintain learners' interest in, and engagement with, the learning process	• video • tutor/mentor evaluation
D2b	Set tasks for learners that will foster their curiosity, creativity and ability to work on their own	• lesson plan • video • tutor/mentor evaluation
D2c	Structure learning in a way likely to foster and maintain learners' enthusiasm and motivation (see D1c)	• lesson plan
D2f	Use a variety of teaching methods to meet the needs of groups and individuals and to provide an environment in which all learners have the opportunity to experience success (H1f)	• lesson plan • video • tutor/mentor evaluation
D2i	Help learners to develop study skills including time management and work organisation skills	• lesson plans • rationales • video • tutor/mentor evaluation
D2j	Encourage learners to take more responsibility for organising their learning successfully (see E2e)	• video • tutor/mentor evaluation • rationale
D3a	Select and organise relevant information clearly and concisely	• lesson plan • video • tutor/mentor evaluation • handouts, OHTs
D3b	Present information to learners clearly and in an appropriate format	• video • tutor/mentor evaluation • resources
D3c	Use a range of communication skills and methods appropriate to specific learners and to the subject being studied	• video • tutor/mentor evaluation • resources
D4b	Give constructive and positive feedback to learners	• video • tutor/mentor evaluation
D5c	Obtain the resources necessary by following the organisation's procedures	• documentation of booking for equipment, such as camera or TV
D5f	Evaluate and ensure the appropriateness and effectiveness of teaching and learning materials and resources for all learners	• lesson rationale • lesson evaluation
D6k	Respond positively and constructively to feedback	• video • tutor/mentor evaluation
D7a	Take responsibility for the quality of service they provide to learners	• journal
D7c	Provide feedback in a form suitable to help measure the quality of learning and teaching	• evaluation • institutional documentation • witness statement
D2c	Promote the concept that learners have a responsibility for ensuring that their learning is successful (see D2j)	• rationale • lesson plan • video • tutor/mentor evaluation
E3d	Liaise with colleagues and other professionals to provide the most effective guidance and support for learners	• witness statement (with examples)
F1a	Identify an appropriate range of assessment methods that will deliver fair, valid and reliable results	• lesson plan • rationale • assessment instruments

F1b	Ensure equality of opportunity in the design and application of assessment procedures	• lesson plan • rationale • assessment instruments
F1c	Ensure that the assessment process, as a whole, is coherent	• lesson plan • rationale • assessment instruments
F1d	Ensure that learners understand the purpose and nature of the assessment process	• video • tutor/mentor evaluation • evaluation
F1e	Create realistic and relevant assessment activities that encourage learning as well as assessing specified outcomes that meet college and external requirements	• plan • rationale • assessment instruments
F1f	Establish the required conditions for assessment and provide the necessary resources	• video • tutor/mentor evaluation
F1g	Use an appropriate variety of valid and reliable assessment procedures that are credible and compatible with the learning programme and the required learning outcomes	• plan • rationale • assessment instruments
F1h	Conduct assessments according to agreed procedures in a fair, consistent and equal manner	• video • tutor/mentor evaluation
F2b	Use assessment info to assess how far learning objectives have been achieved	• lesson evaluation
F2c	Use assessment info in evaluating their own performance as teachers	• evaluation • journal
F2d	Make effective use of assessment information to identify the ways in which teaching might be improved	• evaluation • journal • action plan
G1i	Create and use opportunities to question their own practice and to seek audits of their competence from others, as appropriate	• evaluation • journal • response to tutor/mentor feedback • action plan
G3a	Identify where their own knowledge and skills need to be updated	• evaluation • journal • action plan
H1b	Acknowledge the diversity of learners' experience and support the development needs of individuals (A1a)	• rationale • lesson plan • video • tutor/mentor evaluation
H1c	Are open to different approaches and perspectives on teaching and learning	• journal • rationale and evaluations • response to tutor/mentor feedback
H1d	Develop conditions for learning that are based on mutual respect and trust (B2e)	• video • tutor/mentor evaluation
H1f	Ensure that their own practice promotes equality of opportunity and addresses the needs of all learners (D2f)	• rationale • video • tutor/mentor evaluation • lesson plan
H1h	Use their own experience of learning to inform their approach to teaching	• journal • rationale

H1k	Exercise professional judgement and justify their action in terms of meeting learners' needs	• rationale • evaluation
H2b	Adopt and maintain a professional form of behaviour towards learners and others	• video • witness statement
H2d	Demonstrate responsibility for the effectiveness of education and training and a commitment to the well-being, progress and achievement of learners	• completed documentation • witness statement
H2e	Are aware of and meet their personal responsibilities to learners and others within the framework of the organisation's rules, regulations and duties of care towards learners and others	• witness statement (tutor/mentor)
H2h	Respect the contribution of others to the learning process	• video • tutor/mentor evaluation • witness statement
H2i	Acknowledge the influence of resource constraints and make best professional use of resources and learning opportunities for the benefit of learners	• rationale • video • tutor/mentor evaluation

Intermediate stage: defining the evidence

The skills applicable to the Intermediate stage encompass all those included for the Introductory stage together with the additional skills listed below, which represent and reflect the widening involvement in teaching and learning appropriate to this stage. Much of the suggested evidence is self-explanatory and some, such as the video and tutor/mentor evaluations, have already been discussed in relation to the Introductory stage. Some of the additional sources of evidence suggested here include the following:

Student action plan

This is the plan the student draws up, with your help, as a result of an initial assessment and tutorial. It sets targets and identifies the areas of skills, understanding and knowledge upon which the student particularly needs to focus. It may also identify areas of the learning programme to which the student can bring particular strengths to bear because of past achievements or experience.

Student individual learning plan

Unlike a lesson plan, this is designed for an individual rather than a group. It sets out the learning activities the student will undertake in order to achieve the targets, identified in the action plan.

Scheme of work

The scheme of work is most useful when it takes the form of a series of summarised lesson plans, together with learning materials and materials for assessing whether the planned learning outcomes have been achieved. It will normally cover a module or unit of a particular learning programme and be designed for a specific group of students.

Rationale for scheme of work

Like the rationale for the lesson plan, this sets out the reasons for the way you have selected and sequenced the subject matter and the teaching and learning activities. It will show how you have taken into account the needs and characteristics of the students at whom it is aimed.

Student feedback

Student feedback may be in the form of informal discussion (in which case your evidence will probably be in the written evaluation from your tutor or mentor), or it may be more formalised if you organise written feedback. Some suggestions for ways in which this may be done can be found in Chapter 7.

Your professional action plan

This may be part of your reflective journal. It needs to be regularly updated, and targets from it incorporated into your planning for any teaching and learning session where you will be formally observed by your tutor or mentor.

Evidence of liaison with student support services (SSS)

This demonstrates that you draw upon the student support services in your institution when student needs make this appropriate. The evidence may be in the form of documentation, perhaps, or emails. Alternatively, your tutor or mentor may be able to vouch for this aspect of your professional practice.

Documentation of tutorials

A documentary record of your tutorial sessions with students will contribute to the evidence of the one-to-one support and advice you give to them.

Evidence of your role in the selection and induction of students

These aspects of your practice become more important in the Certification stage, but evidence of some involvement in these procedures is useful at the Intermediate stage, too.

Giving assessment feedback to students

This refers to evidence of written feedback you provide to students following assessment. Evidence of the quality of your spoken feedback to students will be covered in the tutor or mentor evaluations of your practice, video-recordings and student feedback.

A review of current and recent developments in the FE sector

If you are enrolled on a programme of FE teacher training at Intermediate or Certification stage, it is likely you will be asked to produce a review of this kind in some form to demonstrate your familiarity with current policies and practice.

Mapping grid: Intermediate stage

	Skill	Evidence
A1b	Enable learners to review their past experiences in a way that reveals their strengths and weaknesses	• tutorial evidence • student action plans • student individual learning plans • induction evidence
A2c	Consider a range of selection criteria appropriate to learning programmes	• involvement in selection • rationale for scheme of work • journal
A2d	Identify the implications of a disability or learning difficulty for an individual's learning	• student individual learning plan (ILP) • lesson plan • rationale for lesson plan
A2f	Assess the experience, capabilities and learning styles of individual learners in relation to the identified learning programme (see A1b)	• tutorial evidence • student action plans • student ILPs • induction evidence
A2g	Prepare for and carry out initial assessment	• lesson plan • assessment instruments • completed documentation
A2h	Provide feedback to the learner on the outcome of the assessment and its consequences	• record of feedback (oral or written)
A2j	Liaise with colleagues and other interested parties throughout the initial assessment process, as necessary	• minutes of team meetings • completed documentation • tutor/mentor evaluation
B1b	Produce learning outcomes from programmes of study	• lesson plans • schemes of work
B1e	Fulfil validating and awarding bodies' requirements, where relevant	• external verifier's report • internal verifier's report
B2b	Select appropriate teaching techniques to accommodate different styles of learning	• lesson plans • lesson plan rationales • tutor/mentor evaluation • student feedback
B2C	Use individual, small-group and whole-group teaching techniques as appropriate	• lesson plans • lesson plan rationales • tutor/mentor evaluation
B2f	Encourage learners to see the relevance of what they are learning to other aspects of the curriculum and to apply their learning in different contexts	• lesson plans • lesson plan rationales • tutor/mentor evaluation • student feedback
B3c	Contribute to the activities which improve access to the organisation's learning facilities	• tutor/mentor evaluation
B3e	Offer a range of flexible opportunities for learning, including learning facilitated through information learning technology	• lesson plans • examples of use of ILT
C1b	Agree learning goals and targets that support individual needs and aspirations within available resources	• student action plans • student ILPs • tutorial evidence
C1e	Recognise and build on the experiences which learners bring to the programme (see A1b)	• student action plans • student ILPs • tutorial evidence • induction evidence

C1h	Acknowledge the effect of resource constraints and make best use of available opportunities	• lesson plans • lesson plan rationales
C2c	Encourage learning through sound group management including appropriate interventions in group activities	• tutor/mentor evaluations • video
C2d	Facilitate learning through the use of collaborative exercises and encourage learners to support each other	• tutor/mentor evaluation • video • student feedback
C2h	(See C1h)	• lesson plans • lesson plan rationales
C3b	Produce learning plans that encourage learning through experience	• lesson plans
C3d	Encourage and support individuals in identifying personal experiences that enhance their learning (see A1b, C1e)	• student action plans • student ILPs • tutorial evidence • induction evidence
C3g	Provide appropriate constructive feedback to learners and reinforce the learning gained through experience	• feedback to students (oral or written)
C3i	(See C1h, C2h)	• lesson plan • lesson plan rationale
D2d	Match the format and level of learning support materials to the abilities of learners and the desired learning outcomes	• learning materials • lesson plan • lesson plan rationale
D2g	Provide opportunities for learners to reinforce their knowledge and understanding	• lesson plan • lesson plan rationale • tutor/mentor evaluation
D2h	Identify and exploit opportunities to improve learners' basic skills and Key Skills	• lesson plans • tutor/mentor evaluations
D3d	Maintain and encourage effective communication with and between all learners	• tutor/mentor evaluation • video
D3f	Listen to and respond to learners' ideas	• tutor/mentor evaluation • video • student feedback
D4c	Seek and respond appropriately to feedback from learners on their learning	• tutor/mentor evaluation • video • student feedback
D5e	Use IT and learning technology (LT) as appropriate	• lesson plans • examples of IT and LT use
D5g	Help learners to identify appropriate ways of working on their own and provide them with advice and support on using resources effectively	• lesson plans • tutor/mentor evaluation • student feedback • video
D5h	Monitor how learners are responding to teaching and learning materials during the programme and make modifications as necessary	• original teaching and learning materials • student feedback • revised materials • journal
D5j	Keep up to date with the development of resources that enable learners to work effectively on their own	• tutor/mentor evaluation • professional action plan
D6f	Work collaboratively with colleagues to deliver learning programmes	• minutes of team meetings • tutor/mentor reports

E1b	Provide learners with appropriate information about the organisation and its facilities	• induction evidence • student feedback
E1c	Clarify the organisation's expectations of, and obligations to, learners, including the health and safety requirements	• induction evidence • student feedback
E1e	Ensure the learners receive appropriate initial guidance on opportunities for progression	• induction evidence • student feedback
E1g	Evaluate the effectiveness of the induction process with learners	• induction evidence • student feedback
E2a	Provide learners with comprehensive and clear statements of their entitlements and how to access the full range of services available to them	• induction evidence • student feedback
E2b	Ensure that learners are aware of the information facilities and resources available and how to find and use them effectively	• induction evidence • student feedback
E2d	Enable learners to make best use of additional learner support, as appropriate	• evidence of liaison with student support services (SSS) • student feedback
E2e	Promote the concept that learners have a responsibility for ensuring that their learning is successful	• tutor/mentor evaluation • student feedback
E2f	Provide learners with opportunities to consider the next steps after their current programme	• evidence of liaison with SSS (careers) • student feedback • student action plans
E2g	Provide structured opportunities for learners to evaluate and provide feedback on their experience of the organisation	• student feedback • lesson plans
E3b	Contribute to a planned programme of guidance for individual learners	• planned programme, with own contribution(s) identified
E3c	Provide learners with access to additional specialist guidance and support, as required	• evidence of liaison with SSS
E3e	Provide learners with appropriate summative statements of their experiences and achievements when they leave the programme	• examples of summative statements
E4b	Create formal and informal opportunities to listen to and respond to the views and feelings of individual learners (see D3f)	• lesson plans • tutor/mentor evaluations • student feedback
E4d	Know the limits of their own competence as tutors to deal with personal issues	• evidence of liaison with SSS • tutor/mentor evaluations • journal
F1i	Record assessment results, following the organisation's procedures	• completed documentation
F1j	Encourage learners to feel ownership of their assessment records in monitoring and reviewing their own progress	• tutor/mentor evaluation • student action plans • student ILPs
F1k	Ensure that learners are provided with clear and constructive feedback on assessment outcomes within an appropriate timescale	• assessment feedback to students (dated) • student feedback • tutor/mentor evaluation
F2a	Use continuous assessment to help individual learners assess their progress and identify learning issues	• assessment feedback to students • student action plans • student ILPs

F2e	Provide assessment information to appropriate stakeholders	• completed documentation (e.g. for employers)
F2f	Use assessment outcomes in modifying individual learning programmes, as appropriate	• student individual learning programmes (ILPs) • ILP rationales
G1b	Consider their own professional practice in relation to major influences upon FE	• a review of recent and current developments in the FE sector • journal
G1c	Develop opportunities for good practice while recognising the full range of factors and constraints operating within FE	• a review of recent and current developments in the FE sector • journal • lesson plans
G1d	Identify the extent and nature of their current knowledge and skills in relation to the demands of the job	• journal • professional action plan
G1f	Evaluate their own key skills against what is required in their teaching	• journal • action plan
G2a	Identify developments in vocational and educational fields relevant to their own areas of work and to FE in general	• a review of recent and current developments in the FE sector • journal • professional action plan
G2b	Consider the relevance of current developments to their own practice within existing and potential roles	• a review of recent and current developments in the FE sector • journal • professional action plan
G2c	Monitor curriculum developments in their own subject and keep up to date with new topics and new areas of work	• journal • professional action plan
G2d	Take account of subject developments in the content of programmes and in teaching	• lesson plans • schemes of work • tutor/mentor evaluations
G3b	Identify effective ways of maintaining their subject expertise and keeping it up to date	• action plan • evidence of professional development activities
G3d	Set realistic goals and targets for their own development	• professional action plan
H1a	Explore ways of encouraging learners to work effectively on their own and to take more responsibility for ensuring that their learning is successful	• lesson plans • lesson plan rationales • tutor/mentor evaluations • student feedback
H1e	Evaluate how their own practice fosters a desire to learn and enables learners to work effectively on their own and to achieve to the best of their ability	• journal • student feedback
H1j	Work effectively with others to benefit learners	• tutor/mentor evaluations
H2a	Identify an appropriate code of professional practice relevant to the vocational area and FE practice	• tutor/mentor evaluation • journal
H2c	Establish appropriate parameters for professional relationships and exercise judgement as to how best meet learners' needs	• tutor/mentor evaluation • journal
H2f	Meet professional responsibilities in relation to organisational policies and practices	• tutor/mentor evaluation • journal • witness statement
H1g	Represent the organisation in a professional and appropriate manner	• tutor/mentor evaluation • witness statement

Certification stage: defining the evidence

The skills appropriate to the Certification stage include all those already listed for the Introductory and Intermediate stages with the addition of those listed below. The broadening of the teacher's experience at this stage is reflected by the increasing emphasis upon professional values such as inclusiveness and collegiality, and upon the teacher's role in relation to reviewing the quality of provision and providing pastoral care. There is also a greater focus upon the part the teacher plays in encouraging and developing Key Skills and basic skills within the curriculum.

Mapping grid: Certification stage

	Skill	Evidence
A1c	Recognise when additional specialist assessment is required and take the appropriate action	• liaison with SSS • tutor/mentor evaluation
A1d	Support learners while they deal with unfamiliar circumstances and assist learners to explore and articulate their personal aspirations	• induction evidence • student action plans • student ILPs
A1e	Identify and confirm any exemptions to which learners are entitled	• student action plans • student ILPs • APEL documentation
A1f	Provide information to, and negotiate with, colleagues to ensure that the learning needs of individuals can be met in a realistic way	• minutes and memos • tutor/mentor evaluation
A2b	Use a variety of methods for assessing the previous learning experiences and achievements of learners, including their basic skills and Key Skills	• induction evidence • lesson plans • documentation of assessment outcomes
B1f	Ensure that basic skills and Key Skills are integral to provision, as required	• lesson plans • schemes of work • documentation of assessment outcomes
B2d	Set precise targets with individual learners that match their capacities, make the most of their potential for achievement and meet the required learning outcomes	• student action plans • student ILPs
B3a	Maintain contact with those who co-ordinate the links between other institutions and the organisation and across different curriculum areas	• minutes and memos • tutor/mentor report
B3f	Identify and overcome potential barriers to participation in learning programmes	• lesson plans • lesson plan rationales • schemes of work • schemes of work rationales
B3g	Ensure, where possible, within resource constraints, that potential learners are able to experience aspects of the programme before committing themselves to it	• induction evidence • evidence of involvement in selection
B3h	Recognise the organisational and resource constraints influencing participation and make the most of opportunities to achieve wider participation in learning programmes	• scheme of work • evidence of involvement in recruitment/selection
C1a	Establish and agree individual learning needs, aspirations and preferred styles	• student action plans • student ILPs

C1c	Produce learning plans that encourage individual learning	• lesson plans • student ILPs
C1f	Agree learning contract with the learner	• learning contract
C2a	Plan and select learning opportunities that involve group activity	• schemes of work • lesson plans
C3a	Identify learning objectives amenable to learning through experience	• schemes of work • lesson plans
C3c	Plan and structure opportunities for groups and individuals to learn through experience, including opportunities to demonstrate and practise skills	• schemes of work • lesson plan
D2e	Select and develop materials of an appropriate design and format to meet the needs of a wide range of students, including those with hearing or sight impairment	• original learning materials
D3e	Foster learners' enjoyment of learning	• student feedback • video • tutor/mentor evaluation
D4e	Agree appropriate actions with learners	• student action plans
D4f	Consider referral and alternative support networks to assist learners	• liaison with SSS
D4g	Record the outcomes of reviews in accordance with organisational procedures	• completed documentation
D6h	Share expertise with colleagues and respond to their needs, for the benefit of learners and the learning programme	• minutes of course team meetings • tutor/mentor evaluation • witness statement
D6i	Contribute to programme review and evaluation	• minutes of course team meetings • tutor/mentor evaluation
D7e	Identify appropriate data with which to evaluate the quality of the services provided	• student feedback • assessment documentation
D7f	Analyse the information gathered from the evaluation data	• module/course report • minutes of course team meeting
D7h	Use feedback from sources within and outside the organisation in promoting continuous improvement	• module/course report • minutes of course team meeting
E1a	Contribute to the design and implementation of induction procedures	• induction programme, showing own contribution to planning and implementation
E1d	Help learners to gain access to advice and guidance on financial arrangements and personal support	• liaison with SSS
E2c	Provide learners with regular and structured opportunities to review their chosen course of study	• tutorial evidence
E3a	Ensure that learners have access to impartial, comprehensive and current information about training, employment and educational opportunities relevant to their needs and aspirations	• liaison with SSS (careers)
E4a	Provide opportunities for learners to raise personal issues affecting their learning	• tutorial evidence
E4c	Maximise opportunities for learners to have access to specialist support as necessary	• liaison with SSS

E4e	Maintain close and effective links with colleagues and other professionals in order to help individual learners resolve their personal problems	• liaison with SSS • minutes of course team meeting
F1l	Ensure that assessment procedures conform to the organisation's and national requirements, including those of external awarding bodies	• internal verifier report • external verifier report
G1a	Identify where and how their subject or vocational area fits within the organisation and the wider FE sector	• review of recent and current developments in the FE sector
G1e	Conduct a critical evaluation of their own teaching, by eliciting, valuing and using feedback from learners, other teachers, managers and external evaluators	• journal • professional action plan • tutor/mentor evaluation • student feedback
G1g	Evaluate the quality of their relationship with learners, colleagues and other stakeholders	• professional action plan • journal • tutor/mentor evaluation
G1h	Assess their own contribution to the achievement of the organisation's objectives	• professional action plan • appraisal documentation • journal
G1j	Use evaluations to improve their own and their team's effectiveness	• professional action plan • minutes of course team meeting

Mapping the evidence against the standards

The table below demonstrates how, if you are meeting the standards, your preparation, teaching and other aspects of your professional practice will naturally generate evidence this is the case. The majority of the evidence identified here is of this kind. Additional material, such as the review of recent and current developments in FE and the rationales and evaluations of lesson plans and schemes of work, are useful developmental activities which might be undertaken as part of a programme of initial teacher training or continuing professional development.

Mapping grid: evidence and the standards

	Item of evidence	FENTO skill ref.					
1	The record (on video-tape) of a lesson or series of lessons with a group of students	A2a C2d D2f D4b D7c H7d	A2h D2b D2i D6k E2e H7f	B2e D1c D2j D3f F7d H2b	C2e D7b D3a D4c F7f H2h	C3f D7c D3b D5g F7h H2i	C2c D3d D3c D3e H7b
2	Written evaluation by your tutor or mentor of your professional practice. Your responsiveness to this feedback may be demonstrated in your own evaluation of the lesson, which will include, if appropriate, a redrafting of the original lesson plan in the light of your own, and the observer's, evaluations	A1a B2b C2d D2f D3b D4c E2e F1j H1j H2h	A2a B2c C2e D2g D3c D5g E4b F1k H2a H2i	A1c B2e C3f D2h D3d D5j E4d H1a H2c G1e	A1f B2f D1d D2i D3e D6h F1d H1b H2e G1g	A2h B3a D1c D2j D3f D6i F1f H1d H2f G2d	B1b C2c D2b D3a D4b D6k F1h H1f H2g

3	Detailed lesson plans, including those for the sessions observed by the tutor or mentor	A2a A2d A2b A2g B1b B1d B1f B2a B2b B2c B2f B3e B3f B7c C1c C1h C2a C2b C2h C3a C3b C3c C3i D2b D2i D2c D2d D2f D2g D2h D2j D3a D5e D5f D5g E2e E2g E4b F1a F1b F1c F1d F1e F1g G1c G2d H1a H1b H1f H1h H2i
4	Your written rationales for the lesson plans	A1a A2a A2d B1d B2a B2b B2c B2f B3f C1h C2h C3i D2d D2c D2g D2i D2j D5f F1a F1b F1c F1e F1g H1a H1c H1f H1h H1k H2i
5	Your own written evaluations of the teaching and learning sessions which have been observed by your tutor or mentor. The evaluation should demonstrate your responsiveness to the observations made by your tutor or mentor. This may involve a redrafting of the original lesson plan in the light of these	C1g C2g C3h D5f D7c: F1d F2b F2c F2d G1i G3a H1c H1k
6	Copies of all handouts, assessment instruments, OHTs, etc., used in the lesson. These should include examples of your use of information learning technology (ILT)	A2g B3e C1d C2f D2d D2e D3a D3b D3c D5h F1e F1g
7	A reflective journal	A1a A2c A2g D5h D7a E4d F2c F2d G1b G1c G1d G1e G1f G1g G1h G1i G2a G2b G2c G3a H1c H1e H1h H2a H2c H2f
8	Examples of other relevant documentation, such as records of attendance, resource booking forms and records of assessment outcomes	A2b A2g A2j B1f D4g D5c D7e E1f E3e F1i F2e
9	Witness statement completed, signed and dated by the teacher's mentor/tutor/line manager confirming that the teacher has been observed to possess the relevant skills and qualities. These often refer to activities and qualities which become apparent over time and are difficult to demonstrate by use of 'snap-shot' evidence	B3b B3d D6h E3d H2b H2d H2e H2f H2g H2h
10	Student action plan	A1b A1d A1e A2f B2d C1a C1e C3d D4e E2f F1j F2a
11	Student individual learning plan	A1b A1d A1e A2d A2f B2d C1a C1b C1c C1e C3d F1j F2a F2f
12	Scheme of work	B1b B1f B3f B3h C2a C3a C3c
13	Rationale for scheme of work	A2c B3f
14	Student feedback	B2b B2f C2d D3e D3f D4c D5g D5h D7e E1b E1c E1e E1g E2a E2b E2d E2e E2f E2g E4b F1k G1e H1a H1e
15	Professional action plan	D5j G1d G1f G1e G1g G1h G1j G2a G2b G2c G3b G3d G3c
16	Liaison with student support services	A1c D4f E1d E2d E2f E3a E3c E4c E4d E4e
17	Documentation of tutorial support to students	A1b A2f C1b C1e C3d E2c E4a

18	Evidence of role in student selection and induction	A1d E4c	A2b E4d	A2c E4e	A2f	B3g	B3h
19	Assessment feedback to students	A2h	C3g	F1k	F2a		
20	Verifier reports	B1e	F1i				
21	Minutes of team meetings	A1f D6i	A2j D7f	B1e D7h	B3a E4e	D6f G1j	D6h
22	Review of recent and current developments in FE	G1a	G1b	G1c	G2a	G2b	
23	Module/course reports	D7f	D7h				

Useful websites

www.lsagency.org.uk

www.fento.ac.uk